Engaging God's Word

Joshua and Judges

Engage Bible Studies

Tools That Transform

Engage Bible Studies
an imprint of

COMMUNITY
BIBLE STUDY

Contents

Contents

Introduction

Welcome to the life-changing adventure of engaging with God's Word! Whether this is the first time you've opened a Bible or you've studied the Scriptures all your life, good things are in store for you. Studying the Bible is unlike any other kind of study you have ever done. That's because the Word of God is *"living and active"* (Hebrews 4:12) and transcends time and cultures. The earth and heavens as we know them will one day pass away, but God's Word never will (Mark 13:31). It's as relevant to your life today as it was to the people who wrote it down centuries ago. And the fact that God's Word is living and active means that reading God's Word is always meant to be a personal experience. God's Word is not just dead words on a page—it is page after page of living, powerful words—so get ready, because the time you spend studying the Bible in this *Engaging God's Word* course will be life-transforming!

Why Study the Bible?

Some Christians read the Bible because they know they're supposed to. It's a good thing to do, and God expects it. And all that's true! However, there are many additional reasons to study God's Word. Here are just some of them.

We get to know God through His Word. Our God is a relational God who knows us and wants us to know Him. The Scriptures, which He authored, reveal much about Him: how He thinks and feels, what His purposes are, what He thinks about us, how He views the world He made, what He has planned for the future. The Bible shows us God's many attributes—His kindness, goodness, justice, love, faithfulness, mercy, compassion, creativity, redemption, sovereignty, and so on. As we get to know Him through His Word, we come to love and trust Him.

God speaks to us through His Word. One of the primary ways God speaks to us is through His written Word. Don't be surprised if, as you read the Bible, certain parts nearly jump off the page at you, almost as if they'd been written with you in mind. God is the Author of this incredible book, so that's not just possible, it's likely! Whether it is to find comfort, warning, correction, teaching, or guidance, always approach God's Word with your spiritual ears open (Isaiah 55:3) because God, your loving heavenly Father, has things He wants to say to you.

God's Word brings life. Just about everyone wants to learn the secret to "the good life." And the good news is, that secret is found in God's Word. Don't think of the Bible as a bunch of rules. Viewing it with that mindset is a distortion. God gave us His Word because as our Creator and the Creator of the universe, He alone knows how life was meant to work. He knows that love makes us happier than hate, that generosity brings more joy than greed, and that integrity allows us to rest more peacefully at night than deception does. God's ways are not always "easiest" but they are the way to life. As the Psalmist says, *"If Your law had not been my delight, I would have perished in my affliction. I will never forget Your precepts, for by them You have given me life"* (Psalm 119:92-93).

God's Word offers stability in an unstable world. Truth is an ever-changing negotiable for many people in our culture today. But building your life on constantly changing "truth" is like building your house on shifting sand. God's Word, like God Himself, never changes. What He says was true yesterday, is true today, and will still be true a billion years from now. Jesus said, *"Everyone then who hears these words of Mine and does them will be like a wise man who built his house on the rock"* (Matthew 7:24).

God's Word helps us to pray effectively. When we read God's Word and get to know what He is really like, we understand better how to pray. God answers prayers that are according to His will. We discover His will by reading the Bible. First John 5:14-15 tells us that *"this is the confidence that we have toward Him, that if we ask anything according to His will He hears us. And if we know that He hears us in whatever we ask, we know that we have the requests that we have asked of Him."*

How to Get the Most
out of *Engaging God's Word*

Each *Engaging God's Word* study contains key elements that have been carefully designed to help you get the most out of your time in God's Word. Slightly modified for your study-at-home success, this approach is very similar to the tried-and-proven Bible study method that Community Bible Study has used with thousands of men, women, and children across the United States and around the world for nearly 40 years. There are some basic things you can expect to find in each course in this series.

* Lesson 1 provides an overview of the Bible book (or books) you will study and questions to help you focus, anticipate, and pray about what you will be learning.

* Every lesson contains questions to answer on your own, commentary that reviews and clarifies the passage, and three special sections called "Apply what you have learned," "Think about," and "Personalize this lesson."

* Some lessons contain memory verse suggestions.

Whether you plan to use *Engaging God's Word* on your own or with a group, here are some suggestions that will help you enjoy and receive the most benefit from your study.

Spread out each lesson over several days. Your *Engaging God's Word* lessons were designed to take a week to complete. Spreading out your study rather than doing it all at once allows time for the things God is teaching you to sink in and for you to practice applying them.

Pray each time you read God's Word. The Bible is a book unlike any other because God Himself inspired it. The same Spirit who inspired the human authors who wrote it will help you to understand and apply it if you ask Him to. So make it a practice to ask Him to make His Word come alive to you every time you read it.

Read the whole passage covered in the lesson. Before plunging into the questions, take time to read the specific chapter or verses that will be covered in that lesson. Doing this will give you important context for the whole lesson. Reading the Bible in context is an important principle in interpreting it accurately.

Begin learning the memory verse. Learning Scripture by heart requires discipline, but the rewards far outweigh the effort. Memorizing a verse allows you to recall it whenever you need it—for personal encouragement and direction, or to share with someone else. Consider writing the verse on a sticky note or index card that you can post where you will see it often or carry with you to review during the day. Reading and re-reading the verse often—out loud when possible—is a simple way to commit it to memory.

Re-read the passage for each section of questions. Each lesson is divided into sections so that you study one small part of Scripture at a time. Before attempting to answer the questions, review the verses that the questions will cover.

Answer the questions without consulting the Commentary or other reference materials. There is great joy in having the Holy Spirit teach you God's Word on your own, without the help of outside resources. Don't cheat yourself of the delight of discovery by reading the Commentary prematurely. Wait until after you've completed the lesson.

Repeat the process for all the question sections.

Prayerfully consider the "Apply what you have learned," marked with the 📌 push pin symbol. The vision of Community Bible Study is not to just gain knowledge about the Bible, but to be transformed by it. For this reason, each set of questions closes with a section that encourages you to apply what you are learning. Usually this section involves action—something for you to do. As you practice these suggestions, your life will change.

Read the Commentary. *Engaging God's Word* commentaries are written by theologians whose goal is to help you understand the context of what you are studying as it relates to the rest of Scripture, God's character, and what the passage means for your life. Of necessity, the commentaries include the author's interpretations. While interesting and helpful, keep in mind that the Commentary is simply one person's understanding of what these passages mean. Other godly men and women have views that are also worth considering.

Pause to contemplate each "Think about" section, marked with the notepad symbol. These features, embedded in the Commentary, offer a place to pause and consider some of the principles being brought out by the text. They provide excellent ideas to journal about or to discuss with other believers, especially those doing the study with you.

Jot down insights or prayer points from the "Personalize this lesson" marked with the ☑ check box symbol. While the "Apply what you have learned" section focuses on doing, the "Personalize this lesson" section focuses on becoming. Spiritual transformation is not just about doing right things and refraining from doing wrong things—it is about changing from the inside out. To be transformed means letting God change our hearts so that our attitudes, emotions, desires, reactions, and goals are increasingly like Jesus'. Often this section will discuss something that you cannot do in your own strength—so your response will usually be something to pray about. Remember that becoming more Christ-like is not just a matter of trying harder—it requires God's empowerment.

Joshua and Judges Overview

The book of Joshua is the end, the beginning, and the middle of a story. It is a crossing point like the Jordan River itself, a fulcrum on which Israel's history balances and then tips from one side of a promise to the other. Centuries before, God promised Abraham that his descendants would inherit Canaan—the Promised Land. Once Joshua and the Israelites crossed the Jordan and found the promise fulfilled, God gave more commands on how to live there and keep following Him. After their military victory, the people had more work to do. The book of Judges continues the story after the Israelites' victory (and serves as a warning of what could happen after any victory). This next generation of Israelites oscillated from doing evil in the Lord's sight, to crying out to Him for deliverance, and back again. Throughout both books, God identified, called, and used one individual after another, each one custom-fit to take His story to the next page. God used both faithful and flawed people to do what He purposed.

Both Joshua and Judges tell about who God is, who the Israelites were, and what His relationship with them was like. God is a faithful covenant maker and covenant keeper. Joshua watched God make good on the promise He made to Abraham scores of generations before. God is not distant from His people, but He is with us. Not only was He with Joshua and the judges, but He was with His chosen people all along, from long ago. Though this is the story of Joshua and the judges, God reminded His people that Moses before them, and Abraham before Moses, were key players as well. The promise of Canaan was Abraham's, and God promised Joshua, *"Just as I have been with Moses, I will be with you"* (Joshua 1:5).

God accomplished His work through those who obeyed Him and—perhaps surprisingly—those who failed Him. He promised blessing for obedience and knew that His people needed to keep their focus on Him in order to obey His commands, not turning *"to the right or to the left"* (Joshua 1:7). God understood His people's fear. He encouraged them to be strong and courageous as they walked in His ways.

God foresaw His people's weakness in living among the idolatrous Canaanites. After the Israelites obeyed God and took possession of the land, they fell into a whirlpool of rejecting God over and over. While the Lord repeatedly punished them for their sins, He also showed them relentless mercy and delivered them from oppression every time they cried out to Him.

1. Have you ever noticed a spiritual cycle in your life such as the Israelites experienced? What could change a cycle like this?

   _____

   _____

   _____

2. In what areas of your life do you feel a need for more courage and strength? What do you hope to gain from this study as you face these struggles?

   _____

   _____

   _____

If you are doing this study with a group, take time to pray for one another. Ask God to reveal Himself as you work through this study each week, so that you increasingly notice how He cares for each of you and works in your lives. If you are doing this study on your own, ask God to draw you into closer intimacy with Him and to show you how He wants you to live out the lessons in this study.

Joshua: Commissioned by God

As we study the books of Joshua and Judges, we will be inspired by people who made the choice to serve God. Joshua's leadership followed that of the prophet Moses, who led the Hebrews out of Egypt (the Exodus) to Canaan (the Promised Land), a land God pledged to Abraham and his heirs. In the days of Jacob (Abraham's grandson), the Middle East was struck by famine; Jacob and his family migrated to Egypt to survive. Egypt was spared from the famine by the insightful leadership of Jacob's son Joseph, who providentially was sold into Egyptian slavery by his brothers and achieved a position of power there. The Jews stayed in Egypt 430 years until a pharaoh unaware of Joseph's contribution to Egypt enslaved them.

God then chose Moses to lead His people out of this bondage. They journeyed toward Canaan, plagued by problems, but helped by God. Joshua assisted Moses from his youth (Numbers 11:28), and God commissioned him to lead His people after Moses' death.

Joshua's Ancestry and Early Life

Three Old Testament books—Exodus, Numbers, and Deuteronomy— tell of Joshua's early life. In biblical times, names were often significant. Joshua was known as *Hoshea, Yahweh is Helper* (Numbers 13:16), but Moses renamed him *Joshua*, which means *Yahweh saves*, when he joined him in the ministry of liberation. Joshua's parents must have obeyed God's commands when rearing him, nurturing him in the things of God and instilling respect for God's chosen leaders. Their son showed great maturity and Moses gave him responsibility at an early age.

Joshua's Early Commissioning

Joshua's first job as general of the Hebrew army was to fight the

Amalekites. Moses interceded for him during that endeavor; God intervened and Joshua's troops were successful. Moses' prayer and God's answer showed Joshua that God dealt severely with all who opposed Him. This surely helped establish Joshua's faith in his powerful and protective God, a faith necessary if he was to lead the next generation into the Promised Land.

Sometime later, Moses allowed Joshua to accompany him to Mount Sinai, where God's glory rested for six days. To spend this time alone with his beloved teacher, and then to wait for 40 days while Moses entered God's presence, was spiritual training ground for Joshua. As Moses and Joshua returned from the mountain with God's commandments written on stone tablets, Joshua heard *"a noise of war in the camp"* (Exodus 32:15-17). Aaron, convinced that his brother Moses had been gone too long, incited the impatient people into an idolatrous feast, which resulted in Moses' anger and destruction of the tablets.

Joshua's Experience on Mount Sinai

Waiting can be agonizing if filled with doubt and self-pity, or it can be spiritually enriching if done with an attitude of waiting for the Lord. Contrast the actions of Aaron and Joshua, each called to wait for Moses. Aaron was impatient, but Joshua proved himself faithful and trustworthy. He was a man of humility and integrity; he did not boast of his unique experience with Moses. We can see why God chose Joshua as Moses' successor.

The Twelve Spies

When the Israelites reached Kadesh Barnea just north of the Sinai Peninsula, Moses challenged them to possess the land God had promised them, but they were afraid. Rather than trust God's faithfulness, they wanted to see for themselves what was ahead. God had proven Himself utterly trustworthy during their journey; still they were afraid. Moses says, *"'See, the Lord your God has set the land before you. Go up, take possession ... Do not fear or be dismayed.' Then all of you came near me and said, 'Let us send men before us, that they may explore the land for us and bring us word again of the way by which we must go up and the cities into which we shall come'"* (Deuteronomy 1:21-22). Twelve men, one from each of Israel's 12 tribes, were sent to investigate the Promised Land. After 40 days, they returned to Kadesh Barnea with fruit from that area. Ten spies spoke of powerful inhabitants and fortified cities.

At this point Caleb and Joshua tried to persuade the Israelites to trust God and obey His command to inhabit the land. It almost cost them their lives. The people reacted in fear to the discouraging report of the 10 and were ready to stone the two who begged them to trust God. Facing severe disapproval for taking a stand for God must have been hard for Joshua, but it helped him develop into the man who could bring the younger generation into Canaan at the Lord's direction.

Think about how discouragement and disbelief communicate to God that we don't trust Him. We don't believe He is good and His plans are good for us. Caleb and Joshua had great confidence in the Lord. They assured the Israelites, *"The LORD is with us; do not fear them"* (Numbers 14:9). They had seen God's mighty hand and believed He would complete what He had begun. As God's children today, we can have that same confidence in Him, knowing that *"He who began a good work in you will bring it to completion at the day of Jesus Christ"* (Philippians 1:6).

As Moses' assistant helping to govern about 2 million people, Joshua showed his human side. Some elders began to prophesy under the inspiration of God's Spirit. Concerned for Moses' position as a prophet, Joshua asked him to stop the elders from prophesying. Moses responded: *"Are you jealous for my sake? Would that all the LORD's people were prophets, that the LORD would put His Spirit on them!"* (Numbers 11:29). Moses was generous in recognizing others' potential and divine calling. Instead of chastising Joshua, God offered him the opportunity to learn not to be exclusive concerning His spiritual gifts. God knew Joshua's eagerness to learn and his desire to be taught. These qualities made Joshua a good disciple with the potential for being a great leader.

Personalize this lesson.

✓ Like Joshua, we also are called to be God's servants. His commission to those who serve Him is *"Love the LORD your God with all your heart and with all your soul and with all your might"* (Deuteronomy 6:5; Matthew 22:36-38). God is the initiator of love. He came to seek and save us. Who of us could not love the One who has loved us so deeply that He gave His Son so we could have life? His love calls forth from us a response to love Him.

Reflect for a moment on God's love for you. How are you responding to His love? What does it mean for you to love God with all your heart, your soul, and your might? Ask God to help you fully engage with His love so that your service flows from loving God with all you are.

Joshua and Rahab
Joshua 1—2

❖ Joshua 1–2—Joshua and Rahab

1. From chapter 1, with whom did Joshua meet? Why did Joshua meet with them?

_____

_____

2. Who were the principal people in chapter 2?

_____

_____

3. How would you summarize chapter 2 in one sentence?

_____

_____

_____

❖ Joshua 1:1-9—God Places Joshua in Command

4. Why and how did the Lord choose Joshua to lead the Israelites? (See Numbers 27:18-21.)

_____

_____

5. What did God want Joshua to do? What did God promise him?

_____

_____

6. What else did God command (verse 7)?

7. What did God promise if Joshua obeyed these commands?

❖ Joshua 1:10-18—Joshua Organizes the Advance

8. What one word would describe Joshua's response to God?

9. From verses 12-18, why did Joshua direct this group differently than the others? (See Numbers 32.)

10. How did Joshua encourage them?

11. Based on their answer, what was their attitude toward Joshua's leadership?

❖ Joshua 2:1-13—The Two Spies Meet Rahab

12. Who was Rahab? Where did she live?

13. Why were two of Joshua's men in her city?

14. What did Rahab risk by hiding these men?

15. What was Rahab's response to Joshua's men based on?

❖ Joshua 2:14-24—The Spies' Promise

16. What did the men promise Rahab?

17. How did Rahab assist the two men and acknowledge that she believes their promise?

18. What qualified Rahab to be called a servant of God? (See Hebrews 11:31; James 2:25.)

19. What was Rahab's part in biblical history? (See Matthew 1:1-6.)

_____

_____

_____

20. What did you learn about God from this?

_____

_____

_____

_____

_____

Apply what you have learned. God promised Joshua, *"Every place that the sole of your foot will tread upon I have given you … Just as I was with Moses, so I will be with you"* (1:3, 5). Joshua believed God's promise and prepared the people to cross the Jordan River and possess the land. Believing required obedience and action. What promise is God giving you? Do you believe His promise? If so, what action will you take?

Joshua and Rahab
Joshua 1—2

God Chooses and Commissions Joshua

The Israelites completed their desert journey. God did not allow Moses into the Promised Land because of previous disobedience (Numbers 20:7-12). Moses asked God to choose a new leader, *"that the congregation of the LORD may not be as sheep that have no shepherd"* (Numbers 27:17). God appointed Joshua as Israel's new shepherd—not merely their leader in physical battles, but their spiritual leader as well.

God commanded Moses, *"Take Joshua the son of Nun, a man in whom is the Spirit, and lay your hand on him. Make him stand before Eleazar the priest and all the congregation, and you shall commission him in their sight. You shall invest him with some of your authority, that all the congregation of the people of Israel may obey"* (27:18-20).

Think about how God always equips people with His power and wisdom whenever He commissions them to a task. Though Joshua's task was difficult, he had seen God's faithfulness in the past and trusted God's promise for the future. Moses reminded Joshua, *"It is the Lord who goes before you. He will be with you; He will not leave you or forsake you"* (Deuteronomy 31:8). And God Himself told Joshua, *"Be strong and courageous, for you will bring the people of Israel into the land that I swore to give them. I will be with you"* (Deuteronomy 31:23). When God calls you to accomplish a mission, He will equip you just as He did for Joshua.

God Instructs and Assures Joshua

God said, *"Moses My servant is dead. Now therefore arise, go over this Jordan, you and all this people, into the land I am giving to them, to the people of Israel"* (Joshua 1:1-2).

Here God showed His love for Moses. Not until Moses died did God tell Joshua to enter Canaan, so Moses didn't have to watch the Israelites go without him. God also showed His personal interest in Joshua. When God commissioned Joshua to lead the new generation into the Promised Land, He assured him that the land was already theirs (1:3); He gave specific geographical directions; He promised to be with Joshua and assured him that no one would be able to stand against him.

Three times, God commanded Joshua to *"be strong and courageous"* (1:6, 7, 9). The word *strong* comes from the Hebrew word *chazaq, tough.* The word *courageous* is from the Hebrew word *amats, being sharp and confident.* God was saying, "Joshua, be tough, alert, and confident!" God told Joshua to carefully follow the written Law and not to fear or be discouraged, for He would be with him wherever he went.

God told Joshua to constantly read and reflect on this *"Book of the Law"* (known today as the Pentateuch—the first five Old Testament books), urging him to do *"all that is written in it."* The related promise was encouraging: *"Then you will make your way prosperous, and then you will have good success"* (1:8). The word *prosper* is from the Hebrew word *tsalach, to pass through,* which has the sense of moving on and accomplishing one's purpose. How exciting—God linked obedience to His Word with accomplishment and achievement!

Joshua Organizes the Advance

Joshua obeyed God, then urged the young men of the eastern tribes of Reuben and Gad and the half-tribe of Manasseh to join the army. As their commander, Joshua appealed for solidarity. God promised the land to the whole nation of Israel; their unity would create power in itself and allow God to work out His power through them. The people responded, *"All that you have commanded us we will do, and wherever you send us we will go. Just as we obeyed Moses in all things, so we will obey you"* (1:16-17).

Joshua sent two spies to Jericho. Their mission differed from the one almost 40 years earlier when 12 spies explored the land of Canaan (Numbers 13; Deuteronomy 1:19-33). This time strategic military planning, not fear, motivated the expedition. The spies returned with an exciting report: *"Truly the Lord has given all the land into our hands. And also all the inhabitants of the land melt away because of us"* (Joshua 2:24).

Rahab's Faith

The Bible frankly described Rahab as a *"prostitute"* (2:1). We know she had heard of the mighty God of Israel, because her account of Him was accurate (2:8-10). What's more, her actions proved her belief (2:11-14), and she asked the spies to protect her and her entire family when the Israelites took over the city.

Rahab was spiritually sensitive, recognizing the two spies as God's people. She was courageous, risking her life by protecting them. She was resourceful, directing them to safety. She had faith in God and trusted His people. The New Testament author of Hebrews commended her: *"By faith Rahab the prostitute did not perish with those who were disobedient, because she had given a friendly welcome to the spies"* (Hebrews 11:31).

God honored Rahab's action in spite of her being a prostitute. Some might have looked at her background and assumed God would never use her, but *"the Lord sees not as man sees: man looks on the outward appearance, but the Lord looks on the heart"* (1 Samuel 16:7). God had a special plan for Rahab's life. She married Salmon, son of a prince of the tribe of Judah (Numbers 7:12; see Matthew 1:4), and became an ancestress of David and Jesus. *"Salmon the father of Boaz by Rahab, and Boaz the father of Obed by Ruth, and Obed the father of Jesse, and Jesse the father of David the king"* (Matthew 1:5-6). Matthew's genealogy of Christ lists five women: Tamar, who disguised herself as a harlot and became pregnant by her father-in-law, Judah (Genesis 38:12-19); Rahab; Ruth, a Moabitess who migrated to Israel and married Boaz (Ruth 1–4); Bathsheba, who adulterously conceived a baby with David (2 Samuel 11); and Mary, the virgin who became the mother of Jesus (Luke 1:26-27). God worked through them just as they were.

Personalize this lesson.

✓ Obeying God can be scary. Yet the command God gave Joshua (three times!) is our command as well: *"Be strong and courageous."* If Joshua was afraid, his careful obedience to God showed that his faith was greater than his fear. He believed God's promise that He would be with him wherever he went. And he obeyed God's command not to let His words depart from his mouth. If you feel afraid, hesitant, or unwilling to obey God in an area of your life, consider: What do you fear? How does God's promise that He will *"never leave you nor forsake you"* (Hebrews 13:5) counteract that fear? How can you exchange fear for a *"strong and courageous"* faith?

Joshua: Faith and Worship
Joshua 3—5

Memorize God's Word: Joshua 1:9.

❖ Joshua 3:1-6—Joshua Prepares to Cross the Jordan

1. Read Joshua 2:23-24 along with this passage. What do you observe Joshua doing? How could his behavior help you in your own life?

   _____

   _____

   _____

2. What do you think Joshua meant when he said, "*Consecrate yourselves*" (3:5)?

   _____

   _____

3. Why should the people consecrate themselves?

   _____

   _____

4. What is significant about the ark of the covenant? (See Exodus 25:10-22 for further information.)

   _____

   _____

   _____

5. How were the people to follow the ark? What would they gain by following?

    _____

    _____

❖ Joshua 3:7-17—God Once Again Parts the Water

6. Why did God exalt Joshua?

    _____

    _____

7. What is the inherent danger for any leader God has lifted up, whether in Bible times or today? What could a leader do to avert that danger? (See Isaiah 42:8; Psalm 115:1.)

    _____

    _____

8. When Joshua spoke to the people of Israel, how did he exalt the Lord?

    _____

    _____

9. When did God part the Jordan waters?

    _____

    _____

❖ Joshua 4:1-11—The People Set Up a Memorial

10. Whom did the twelve men represent? (See Joshua 3:12.) What did Joshua direct them to do?

    _____

    _____

11. What reasons did he give for these directions?

    _____

    _____

12. How would future generations benefit?

_____

_____

13. What has God done in your life that would inspire you to establish a memorial to His power and faithfulness?

_____

_____

_____

_____

14. What could your "*stone memorial*" look like?

_____

_____

❖ Joshua 4:12–5:1—The Israelites Arrive in the Promised Land

15. When and how did the Jordan River flow again?

_____

_____

16. When children of future generations asked about the stone memorial, what were the fathers to tell them? What truths about God were they to teach?

_____

_____

_____

_____

17. Whom does God want you to influence and teach? What are you to teach them?

_____

_____

_____

❖ Joshua 5:2-15—Joshua Renews Rituals and Celebrations

18. Why did Joshua circumcise the male Israelites?

_____

_____

19. What did circumcision signify? (See Genesis 17:9-11.)

_____

_____

20. Read Romans 2:29, Philippians 3:3, and Colossians 2:11-12. How do these New Testament verses explain or describe circumcision? How do these verses change, solidify, or shed more light on your own understanding of circumcision?

_____

_____

21. According to Exodus 12:21-27, why should the Israelites observe the Passover?

_____

_____

_____

_____

_____

Apply what you have learned. God's presence humbled and awed Joshua and Moses. Both removed their shoes to signify reverence and worship to God. What physical signs might help you express your own awe and humility as you worship almighty God?

Joshua: Faith and Worship
Joshua 3—5

Stepping Out in Faith

Joshua sent two men to spy out the long-awaited land God promised their forefathers. They came back to report, *"Truly the LORD has given all the land into our hands"* (Joshua 2:24)—the Promised Land they had been waiting for. Joshua and the Israelites left the very next morning.

The ark of the covenant went with them. It symbolized God's glory and reminded the Israelites that God went before them, God was with them, and God was near. The ark was in the Most Holy Place (Exodus 26:33) and contained three items: manna, Aaron's rod, and the two tablets of God's commandments (Hebrews 9:4). The Levitical priests were to carry the ark while the Israelites followed a thousand yards behind.

Joshua told the people to *"consecrate"* themselves, which included washing their garments, eating only permitted foods, putting away foreign gods, purifying themselves (probably ritualistically), and changing their garments. Then they would be sanctified, set apart for God, prepared for an audience with Him.

With his God-affirmed leadership (3:7), Joshua told the people to *"come here and listen"* to what they needed to know. God would drive out the Canaanites. God's presence in the ark would go before them. And a delegate from each tribe would see the Jordan waters miraculously stand aside.

Miracle at the Jordan

Every harvest season, the Jordan swelled and overflowed its banks. As soon as the priests carrying the ark dipped their feet into the river, the water stopped flowing and *"rose up in a heap"* far upstream (3:16). The river flow ceased, and the people crossed over.

With the river at flood stage, crossing would have been impossible, but nothing is impossible with God. The priests stood in the dry riverbed while everyone else went across. Like their parents in Moses' time, this generation of Israelites must have been awestruck by God's power and provision.

Think about how Joshua's knowledge of God's trustworthiness fueled his courage and obedience. He focused on God above, not the swirling waters below. When we can't think of a solution to our problems, that doesn't mean there is none, for God is more than we know or can imagine (Ephesians 3:20-21). When God brings us to the brink of turbulence, can we walk by faith with Him? God's Word says the one who trusts Him is blessed (Psalm 40:4), and He will never leave or forsake us (Hebrews 13:5).

The 12 Memorial Stones

After all the people crossed over, God told Joshua, *"Take twelve men from the people, from each tribe a man, and command them, saying, 'Take twelve stones from here out of the midst of the Jordan, from the very place where the priests' feet stood firmly, and … lay them down in the place where you lodge tonight'"* (4:2-3). These stones would remind the Israelites and future generations of God's mighty acts and His care for His people. The priests bearing the ark waited patiently in the riverbed until God commanded them to come out. When they did, the river again flowed, flooding its banks as before. The testimony of God's power went beyond Israel; when the Canaanite kings heard about this miracle, *"their hearts melted"* in fear.

The People Circumcised

Two important events happened at Gilgal: circumcision and the Passover celebration. This was the first Passover the nation observed in the Promised Land, and the people could not celebrate until the males were circumcised (Exodus 12:48). So God charged Joshua, *"Make flint knives and circumcise the sons of Israel"* (5:2).

The Israelites had observed the first Passover on the night before they left

Egypt—the 10th day of the first month. God chose this same date years later to part the Jordan River and usher the Israelites into the Promised Land. The water had parted at the beginning of their journey and now at the end. The wilderness wandering was over. How appropriate for them to celebrate the Passover again before taking possession of the land.

But why would God require circumcision? Circumcision was a sign of God's covenant with Abraham and his offspring (Genesis 17:9-14). It clearly marked them as the Lord's, setting them apart from other people groups. No infant boy born in the desert had been circumcised (5:4-7), so they obeyed, and God approved: *"Today I have rolled away the reproach of Egypt from you"* (5:9). For this generation, circumcision also symbolized their freedom from slavery in Egypt.

Think about the New Testament emphasis on circumcision: an inward, spiritual condition that is the Holy Spirit's work. God requires internal change: our heartfelt devotion and obedience to Him. When true circumcision becomes a reality to us, we can worship God by His Spirit. Then we will be truly free from to sin, fleshly passions, or the call of this world—even as God freed the Israelites from their bondage in Egypt.

God instituted the Passover Feast in Egypt, right before the Exodus (Exodus 12:3-49). The Passover celebrated the night God saved the enslaved Israelites by directing the angel of death to pass over homes with lamb's blood painted on their doorposts. Today it still symbolizes the redemptive blood of a lamb—the Lamb of God who takes away our sins. Jesus is the Passover Lamb sacrificed for the sin of the world (1 Corinthians 5:7).

Personalize this lesson.

✓ After the Passover, God appeared to Joshua in the form of a man *"standing before him with his drawn sword in his hand. And Joshua went to him and said to him, 'Are you for us, or for our adversaries?'"* (5:13). The man said he commanded the Lord's army and had come to Joshua and his army. Joshua responded by bowing face down in worship. The "man" allowed Joshua to show Him reverence indicating this may have been a theophany—a pre-incarnate appearance of the Lord Jesus Christ. He told Joshua, *"Take off your sandals from your feet, for the place where you are standing is holy"* (5:15). The Lord Himself came to Joshua just like He had come to Moses. Like Moses, Joshua responded with worship.

Joshua: Trust and Victory
Joshua 6—8

Memorize God's Word: Proverbs 3:5-6.

❖ Joshua 6:1-14—God's Plans for Jericho's Defeat

1. Why were Jericho's gates shut and guarded? What did this indicate about Israel's military position?

   _____

   _____

2. What was God's plan for conquering Jericho?

   _____

   _____

3. How did Joshua respond to God's instructions?

   _____

   _____

❖ Joshua 6:15-27—Jericho's Destruction

4. What happened on the seventh day?

   _____

   _____

5. What was to be destroyed and what was to be saved?

   _____

   _____

6. According to Hebrews 11:30, what, in one word, was the means of victory? How can you apply this same word to your own "battles"?

    _____

    _____

    _____

7. Whom did Joshua send to rescue Rahab? Why do you think Joshua chose them?

    _____

    _____

8. Who else besides Rahab was spared because of her faith (see verses 17 and 23)?

    _____

    _____

❖ Joshua 7:1-9—First Battle at Ai

9. Review Joshua 6:17-19 with Joshua 7:1. Who was to receive all goods taken from Jericho? Who violated these instructions, and how?

    _____

    _____

    _____

10. What consequences did Joshua give for such disobedience? How did it affect Israel?

    _____

    _____

11. How did the Israelites attempt to conquer Ai? What was the outcome?

    _____

    _____

12. How did Joshua react to this defeat? What was his major concern?

_____

_____

❖ Joshua 7:10-26—Achan's Sin Uncovered and Removed

13. When God spoke to Joshua, what did He reveal and explain about Israel's trouble? What action did God demand?

_____

_____

_____

14. What did Joshua challenge Achan to do?

_____

_____

15. What was Achan's sentence and punishment?

_____

_____

16. What parts of the story might indicate why God pronounces such strong judgment? What was God's response after the judgment?

_____

_____

_____

_____

❖ Joshua 8:1-35—Second Battle at Ai

17. How did God prepare Joshua to defeat Ai?

_____

_____

18. What was Joshua's sign to begin the ambush? The Israelites attacked the men of Ai after seeing what other sign?

_____

_____

19. God gave the Israelites the spoils from Ai but not from their first victory at Jericho. What parts of each story might indicate why?

_____

_____

20. Moses' words in Deuteronomy 11:26-28 sum up all that Joshua read to the people at Mount Gerizim and Mount Ebal. What were the consequences of their obedience and disobedience? (See also Deuteronomy 28.)

_____

_____

_____

_____

Apply what you have learned. Take a moment to write down some words that immediately come to mind when you think of the word "obedience." Jesus said, *"If you keep My commandments, you will abide in My love, just as I have kept My Father's commandments and abide in His love. These things I have spoken to you, that My joy may be in you, and that your joy may be full"* (John 15:10-11). God's Word in Deuteronomy associates obedience with blessing. And Jesus made a direct link between obedience and His love and joy! Do you find it hard to obey God in a specific area right now? If so, consider how obeying Him in this could lead to the blessings, love, and joy He wants for you.

Joshua: Trust and Victory
Joshua 6—8

Occupying Jericho

The Israelites crossed the Jordan. Before them was Canaan, the long-awaited Promised Land that God had sworn to give their fathers. Joshua led the way commissioned by God's command to be strong and courageous. First, they conquered Jericho. God armed Joshua with specific instructions and a promise: *"See, I have given Jericho into your hand, with its king and mighty men of valor. You shall march around the city"* (6:2-3).

Believers today also have a clear mandate from Christ: *"You will receive power when the Holy Spirit has come upon you, and you will by My witnesses in Jerusalem and in all Judea and Samaria, and to the end of the earth"* (Acts 1:8). The Lord promised to be with Joshua as he obeyed specific commands. This is also true for us if we trust and obey.

Joshua carefully followed God's orders, though they were unconventional and may have seemed impractical from a military standpoint. He recruited the Levitical priests to bear trumpets of rams' horns and to carry the ark of the Lord (6:6; see also Numbers 10:8-9). He put armed guards before and behind the trumpeters (6:8-9). He told the people to follow the rear guard in absolute silence—not a single word (6:10)—while the rams' horns blew non-stop.

The whole procession circled the city wall once a day, six days in a row. On the seventh day they circled seven times, trumpets still sounding. But the last time around, they made noise—*"The people shouted a great shout, and the wall fell down flat"* (6:20).

Rahab told the two spies, "the fear of you has fallen upon us" (2:9). Those in the city shut it up *"inside and outside"* (6:1). How frightened they must have been as Israel marched around their city, day after day. On the seventh day, according to God's promise, the wall collapsed, and they burned the city as an offering to Him. In obedience, they dedicated Jericho to God for its destruction, giving the spoil to the Lord's treasury as sacred objects.

Think about how Joshua did not trust in human strength or skill. He listened to God's battle plan and trusted God, the true Conqueror, to give victory. And God did! God calls us to trust Him with all our hearts and not to rely on our limited understanding (Proverbs 3:5) His understanding is infinite, (Psalm 147:5) and we can trust Him to act (Psalm 37:5). When we trust God and His plans completely, we will recognize that what we achieve is not by our own might or knowledge but by His power and wisdom.

After taking over Jericho, Joshua charged the two spies to rescue Rahab and her family. Rahab was willing to forsake her own people to become a part of God's community. Because of Rahab's decision, she became an ancestress of King David and Jesus Christ. What a merciful God we have! Despite Rahab's earlier failures, the Lord counted her righteous along with Abraham because she turned to Him in faith.

Achan Ignores God's Instructions

God wanted everything gained from Jericho—the silver and gold, and all bronze or iron vessels—to be dedicated to His treasury. Joshua relayed God's explicit command to the people; violation meant death. But Achan defied God, and the whole nation suffered humiliating defeat. Achan was sentenced to die, and his family died with him.

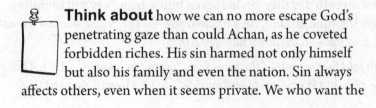

Think about how we can no more escape God's penetrating gaze than could Achan, as he coveted forbidden riches. His sin harmed not only himself but also his family and even the nation. Sin always affects others, even when it seems private. We who want the best for our loved ones as well as our larger communities should heed God's words: *"If My people who are called by My name humble themselves, and pray and seek My face and turn from their wicked ways, then I will hear from heaven and will forgive their sin and heal their land"* (2 Chronicles 7:14).

After the defeat at Ai, Joshua and the elders tore their clothes, fell on their faces, and covered their heads with dust. Joshua cried out to God and asked why He had brought them over the Jordan only to give them to their enemies. God responded by telling him to consecrate the people. God's policy had not changed: disobedience brought curse and defeat.

The Battle for Ai

God dealt with the sin and then promised Israel victory over Ai. Joshua obeyed His counsel and lured Ai's men out of the city. What a contrast to the earlier defeat! God was indeed with them. And *"if God is for us, who can be against us?"* (Romans 8:31).

In gratitude, Joshua built an altar on Mount Ebal to remind the Israelites of their obligation to God. The altar was made of uncut stones so no one could boast that it was his own work. They were to stand before the two mountains, Mount Ebal and Mount Gerizim, where the crowd could hear Joshua's voice. Joshua built the altar not on Gerizim, from which blessings were declared, but from Ebal, the place of pronounced curses.

To reach for blessings before coming to repentance is to deceive ourselves. The mountains Gerizim and Ebal powerfully remind us that God's redemption is for sin and its consequences. Before we stand on Gerizim's blessings, we must first *face* our sins and repent at "Ebal." There, we accept God's forgiveness that comes only by way of His altar, the cross where His Son died as *"an atoning sacrifice for our sins"* (1 John 4:10, NIV).

The Samaritans later chose Mount Gerizim, not Mount Ebal, as their place of worship. But Jesus didn't tell the Samaritan woman to worship at Mount Gerizim or at Jerusalem. He defined true worship of the Father through the one who would die for all men's sins: *"Woman, believe Me, the hour is coming when neither on this mountain nor in Jerusalem will you worship the Father. ... God is spirit, and those who worship Him must worship in spirit and truth"* (John 4:21, 24).

Personalize this lesson.

✓ The battles of Jericho and Ai are a stark contrast to each other. God led the battle against Jericho down to the most precise detail. Joshua obeyed the explicit instructions and the conquest was triumphant. Then, without mention of seeking God's direction, Joshua led the attack on Ai. He dispatched the spies and followed their advice. Ai soundly defeated the 3,000 Israelite warriors. God had removed His blessing from Israel because of Achan's sin and Joshua was unaware. He mourned and cried out to God afterward. God responded to Joshua, *"Israel has sinned … Therefore the people of Israel cannot stand before their enemies"* (7:11-12). What if Joshua would have sought God about the attack on Ai? How do you think the story might have been different? Checking in with God is a humble acknowledgment that He knows what we do not know. How can you build into your life the discipline of checking in with God for His direction for you?

Joshua: Justice and Power
Joshua 9—12

❖ Joshua 9:1-15—A Deceptive Pact

1. The kings mentioned in verse 1 governed which people groups? What did these kings do after hearing about Israel's military successes?

   _____

   _____

   _____

2. What steps did the Gibeonites take to deceive the Israelites?

   _____

   _____

   _____

3. What did they say to Joshua?

   _____

   _____

   _____

4. What did Israel do in response? What did they not do?

   _____

   _____

   _____

   _____

❖ Joshua 9:16-27—Joshua Punishes the Gibeonites

5. How long did it take the Israelites to find out about the Gibeonites' deception? Where did they go to settle this matter?

_____

_____

6. Why did the Israelites keep their promise even though they were deceived? (See Deuteronomy 23:21.)

_____

_____

7. Why did the Gibeonites deceive Israel?

_____

_____

8. What was their punishment? How might this benefit both the Israelites and the Gibeonites?

_____

_____

❖ Joshua 10:1-15—Israel Defeats the Amorites

9. How does this passage describe Gibeon and its people?

_____

_____

10. Who attacked Gibeon? Why?

_____

_____

11. Why did Joshua and his men enter this war?

_____

_____

12. In what specific ways did God help Joshua?

❖ Joshua 10:16-43—Joshua Completes Central and Southern Campaigns

13. To where did the five kings flee? How did Joshua confine them there?

14. When all the Israelites returned safely, what did Joshua tell his chiefs to do with the five kings?

15. What did Joshua tell the people about God (10:19,25; see also verse 42)?

❖ Joshua 11–12—Israel Seizes Northern Canaan

16. What did King Jabin do when he heard about Israel's victories in southern Canaan?

17. Which Canaanite kings are listed in 11:1-3?

18. What were their combined armies like?

19. Why did Joshua treat the conquered Canaanites as he did? (See 11:6; Deuteronomy 7:1-5; 20:16-18.)

_____

_____

_____

Apply what you have learned. The Israelites personally confronted the Gibeonites who had wronged them. Confronting people takes courage! Do you currently have a disagreement with someone? How can you follow Joshua's example with the Gibeonites? What next steps should you take in this relationship? (See also Matthew 5:23-34; 18:15-17.)

Joshua: Justice and Power
Joshua 9—12

When the Israelites entered Canaan, they were the living fulfillment of God's promise to the patriarchs and to Moses. God promised to give Abraham's descendants the land of Canaan. Moses led the people to the Jordan, north of the Dead Sea. God appointed Joshua to lead the people on into the land. With the crumbling of Jericho's wall, the divine purification at Ai, and the lesson at Mount Ebal, the Israelites learned that God's victories must be won God's way. From their camp in central Canaan they would conquer first the south (chapters 9-10) and then the north (11:1-15).

A Deceptive Pact

The southern kings formed a wartime coalition. The Gibeonites, however, knew of God and feared Him—so they devised a different plan. The Gibeonites disguised some men as people *"from a distant country"* (9:3-6), sending them out to meet Joshua at his camp. With their old clothes and moldy food, they convinced the Israelites that their story of a long journey was true.

Instead of consulting God, the Israelites foolishly made a pact with the Gibeonites, which later caused problems for them. Because Joshua had committed to protect Gibeon, his men joined the Gibeonites' fight against the Amorite coalition. Although the people murmured against the leaders, Joshua refused to break his covenant with the Gibeonites because that would have been a sin directly against the Lord in whose name they had sworn.

Although the Israelites wanted to kill the Gibeonites, Joshua would not allow it. Instead, he ordered that the Gibeonites serve as wood choppers and water carriers for the tabernacle. Although Joshua calls this arrangement a "curse," there is mercy in it (see Psalm 84:10).

Allocated to Aaron's descendants when Joshua divided the land (Joshua 21:17-19), Gibeon would become a special place of worship, the home of God's tabernacle and an altar for burnt offerings (1 Chronicles 21:29). King Solomon later offered sacrifices there and received God's promise of wisdom, riches, and honor. Five hundred years after Solomon, the Gibeonites helped Nehemiah rebuild the walls of Jerusalem. Joshua used poor judgment in making that treaty, yet God worked good out of Joshua's error.

God on the Battlefront

Despite Joshua's mistake, God was faithful and assured him victory. Humanly speaking the odds were poor: five kingdoms against two. Yet Joshua saw the odds as great: almighty God against five small kingdoms! So he obeyed God, marching from Gilgal into battle that night. *"The LORD threw them into a panic before Israel, who struck them with a great blow at Gibeon"* (10:10), even throwing giant hailstones on them so that *"there were more who died because of hailstones than the sons of Israel killed by the sword"* (10:11).

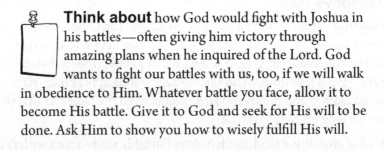

Think about how God would fight with Joshua in his battles—often giving him victory through amazing plans when he inquired of the Lord. God wants to fight our battles with us, too, if we will walk in obedience to Him. Whatever battle you face, allow it to become His battle. Give it to God and seek for His will to be done. Ask Him to show you how to wisely fulfill His will.

As Joshua fought the Amorites, he spoke to the Lord and God granted his prayer for extra light: *"the sun stood still, and the moon stopped, until the nation took vengeance on their enemies"* (Joshua 10:13). The phrase *"the sun stood still"* does not prove the author to be scientifically ignorant or the text inaccurate. Although we know today that the earth spins around the sun, which stays in one place, thus producing day and night, we still speak of the sun "setting" or "rising." We should view this miracle with thankfulness rather than theorizing, because only the God who performed this miracle knows the details.

It must have been hard for Joshua to destroy all that breathed, as God commanded. Because he was obeying God, we need to examine the reason for such harsh measures. The Bible is explicit about the Canaanites' depraved condition. (See Deuteronomy 12:29-31). Archaeological findings confirm their debased form of polytheism (worship of many gods) in ritual fertility cult worship. Some of their deities were: El, leader of their gods; Anath, the "sacred prostitute"; Astarte, goddess of the evening star; Asherah, goddess of the sea and El's consort; and Baal, the god of fertility who succeeded El as king. Archaeologists have also unearthed an Anath worship center at Gebal in Phoenicia. Anath was the goddess of violence and war; all the images uncovered there were of a sexual nature. Their temple worship included fertility rites, "sacred" prostitution, child sacrifice, and snake worship—all abominations in God's sight.

The Lord had warned the Israelites through Moses: *"Do not make yourselves unclean by any of these things, for by all these the nations I am driving out before you have become unclean, and the land became unclean, so that I punished its iniquity, and the land vomited out its inhabitants"* (Leviticus 18:24-25). God repeatedly emphasized the danger of Canaanite influence. Sin caused many to perish. In Noah's days, God sent a flood; He consumed Sodom and Gomorrah with fire. Now God used hail and the Israelites to bring judgment on the Canaanites.

The Land Rests From War

In Moses' days, the Israelites captured the region east of the Jordan River. They defeated Sihon, the Amorite king of Heshbon, and King Og of Bashan. Then Joshua and his men occupied the Promised Land west of the Jordan. (See Joshua 12.) The Israelites defeated 31 kings west of the Jordan River. It took Joshua and his army about seven years to conquer the main region of Canaan. Entry into the Promised Land required great patience, spiritual sensitivity, wisdom, and unity. God said He would grant the Promised Land to Israel, but they had to work to gain it. Their labor was not in vain. In our own spiritual pilgrimages, God calls us to claim what He has promised us and to *"be steadfast, immovable, always abounding in the work of the Lord, knowing that in the Lord your labor is not in vain"* (1 Corinthians 15:58).

Personalize this lesson.

✓ Joshua kept his oath to the Gibeonites even though they had lied to him. If someone tricked you into making a promise, how would you react? When someone deceives us, most of us don't feel obligated to keep our word. But Psalm 15:4 offers blessing for the person *"who keeps an oath even when it hurts, and does not change their mind."* The power of integrity is that our response is not determined by how others treat us. When someone lies to us, we can choose to be trustworthy. When others break their word, ours can remain unbroken. Are you facing a specific situation right now that calls you to deeper integrity? Talk with God about how you can maintain your integrity in difficult circumstances.

Joshua: Obedience and Peace
Joshua 13—21

Memorize God's Word: Deuteronomy 6:18a.

❖ Joshua 13:1–14:5—Dividing the Land

1. How did God continue to use Joshua in his old age (Joshua 13)?

   _____

   _____

2. What advantages might an older person have in serving God?

   _____

   _____

   _____

3. What land was given to nine-and-a-half tribes? To two-and-a-half tribes? To the Levites? (See also Numbers 33:54; Joshua 13:14.)

   _____

   _____

   _____

❖ Joshua 14:6-15; 15:13-19—Caleb's Reward

4. Earlier in Caleb's life, who appointed him to a special task? How old was he at that time?

   _____

   _____

5. What was the task? How had he performed it?

    _____

    _____

6. How old was Caleb at the time of this passage? How did he describe himself?

    _____

    _____

7. What did he propose to Joshua? What was Joshua's response?

    _____

    _____

8. What words describe Caleb's character?

    _____

    _____

    _____

❖ Joshua 18; 19:49-51—The Tent of Meeting at Shiloh

9. Who gathered at Shiloh? How did they show their priorities (what did they do first)?

    _____

    _____

10. Why might they have chosen Shiloh for the tent of meeting? What was there before? (See also 1 Samuel 4:3-4; Hebrews 9:4-5.)

    _____

    _____

11. How did Joshua exhort the people? What did he command?

    _____

    _____

12. Where did Joshua settle? What circumstances made his inheritance possible?

_____

_____

❖ Joshua 20; 21:1-3, 41-42—Cities of Refuge, Cities of Priests

13. What was the purpose for the cities of refuge?

_____

_____

14. What were the six cities of refuge? What do you note about their distribution?

_____

_____

_____

15. From Deuteronomy 18:1-5, what was the nature of the Levites' inheritance? How did God meet their needs?

_____

_____

16. How did God establish the Levitical cities? How many were there?

_____

_____

❖ Joshua 21:3-45—God Fulfills His Promise

17. What did God promise Israel? What was the outcome of these promises?

_____

_____

_____

18. What would help grow your faith while you are waiting for God to fulfill His promise?

_____

_____

_____

Apply what you have learned. God used Joshua and Caleb when they were young and when they were old. You, today, are older than you were and younger than you will be. How can you make yourself available to God now in a way that you may not be able to later? How can God use you now in a way He didn't use you before? God can make you fruitful at any age! (Consider 1 Timothy 4:12 and Psalm 92:14.) Ask God how He wants you to serve Him in this season.

Joshua: Obedience and Peace
Joshua 13—21

God continued entrusting Joshua with mission and purpose in his older years. Though Joshua's army did overcome both southern and northern Canaanites, they hadn't yet possessed all the land. Confident because of God's promises, Joshua didn't hesitate to execute God's command—allocating all of Canaan to Israel's 12 tribes (chapters 13–21).

Then the Israelites became complacent. They didn't *"drive out all the inhabitants from the land"* (Numbers 33:51-53) but allowed some Canaanites to remain. Joshua challenged the Israelites by asking how long they would wait before obeying God's command to take the land. He knew disaster would accompany their disobedience (Numbers 33:54-56). As God forewarned, their involvement with Canaanites caused a long and painful struggle. Even Israel's most powerful king, David, couldn't deliver Israel from the Canaanite tribes' ongoing attacks. Indeed, to disobey God is to invite trouble.

The Faithful Caleb

In the midst of the conquest and the tribes of Israel receiving their land allotments, Caleb approached Joshua. The two faithful friends had earlier spied out this land at Moses' order (Numbers 13:1-33). Only Caleb and Joshua trusted God to give Israel the Promised Land. Now 85 years old, Caleb asked Joshua for the land Moses promised him and for permission to take over the country of the Anakim (14:10-12). Joshua granted his requests.

Age didn't diminish God's plan for Caleb. He was still as strong and healthy as he was in Moses' time and could testify with the psalmist, *"I have been young, and now am old, yet I have not seen the righteous forsaken or his children begging for bread"* (Psalm 37:25). Caleb faithfully walked with God and trusted Him. If we seek to walk in God's path prepared for us, we will have His help. *"The steps of a man are established by the* LORD, *when He delights in his way; though he fall, he shall not be cast headlong, for the* LORD *upholds his hand"* (Psalm 37:23-24).

Establishing the Tabernacle

The Israelites set up the tent of meeting (tabernacle) in Shiloh—a central undertaking, as it was their first worship center in the Promised Land. Later a temple in Jerusalem would serve as a permanent worship place.

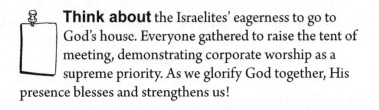

Think about the Israelites' eagerness to go to God's house. Everyone gathered to raise the tent of meeting, demonstrating corporate worship as a supreme priority. As we glorify God together, His presence blesses and strengthens us!

Dividing the Land

Joshua told the men to survey the land *"and return to me. And I will cast lots for you here before the* LORD *in Shiloh"* (Joshua 18:8). God sovereignly used that method to allocate the land fairly to all the tribes, including families that had only daughters (17:1-6).

No one was left out or received a disproportionate amount. Reuben, Gad, and the half-tribe of Manasseh received territory east of the Jordan; Judah, under Caleb's influence, received the hill country west of the Jordan; Ephraim and the other half-tribe of Manasseh received regions west of the Jordan; and the final seven tribes received territory on the west side.

While he delegated those parcels of land, Joshua could have kept the best portion for himself, but he did not. Therefore, the people gave him Timnath-serah in Ephraim as God commanded.

Joshua fought long and hard for God and his people. He led successfully because he obeyed God's command: *"This Book of the Law shall not depart from your mouth, but you shall meditate on it day and night, ... For then you will make your way prosperous, and then you will have good success"* (Joshua 1:8).

Cities of Refuge, Cities of Priests

The Promised Land was to have six cities of refuge, three on the west side of the Jordan (Kedesh in Galilee; Shechem in Ephraim; and Hebron in Judah) and three on the east side (Bezer in Reuben; Ramoth in Gad; and Golan in Manasseh) (20:7-8). These cities belonged to the Levites and provided protection for anyone who had accidentally killed another. (See Deuteronomy 19:5.)

The concept of cities of refuge shows that the Mosaic Law afforded a way of showing mercy while fulfilling the strict requirements of justice. The idea of the cities of refuge parallels God's provision for us in His Son Jesus Christ. (See Hebrews 6:18-20.) There is a difference, however: Jesus' redemptive ministry provides anyone the opportunity to experience God's grace, while the cities of refuge only protected those who had committed unintentional crimes. Also, only a few cities of refuge existed at various locations, but Jesus Christ is available for all who need Him: *"Since then we have a great high priest who has passed through the heavens, Jesus, the Son of God, ... Let us then with confidence draw near to the throne of grace, that we may receive mercy and find grace to help in time of need"* (Hebrews 4:14, 16).

There were three clans of Levites: Kohath, Gershon, and Merari. Moses set apart 48 towns with pastureland as their dwelling places, but they received no inheritance. *"To the tribe of Levi alone Moses gave no inheritance. The offerings by fire to the LORD God of Israel are their inheritance, as He said to him"* (Joshua 13:14; see Deuteronomy 18:1-8). How did they manage to live without agricultural lands? According to the Pentateuch, they received the people's tithes. God told Aaron that He gave the Levites *"every tithe in Israel for an inheritance, in return for their service ... in the tent of meeting"* (Numbers 18:21). In order not to be burdened by earthly tasks while serving God in the tabernacle and ministering to the people's spiritual needs, the Levites had the set-apart portions that belonged to the Lord. At the same time, they were to share their tithes with Aaron the priest and to present an offering to the Lord.

Personalize this lesson.

✓ God set up the ancient system of cities of refuge. All of us have sinned—intentionally or not—and need a refuge. In Joshua's day, those who had sinned had to run or hide or suffer the penalty of death. It's not much different for us. Our sin—intentional or not—brings God's judgment on us. We experience death in our relationships with each other and with God. But Jesus is our place of refuge. Because of His death, we can take refuge in Him. Where in your life are you experiencing death? In your relationships? With God? In your innocence? Your integrity? Don't flee or hide from your Refuge. Instead, confess your sin to God. Believe and accept His forgiveness. And walk into life with Jesus. You may want to talk with a mature Christian friend if you need help.

Joshua: Loving and Honoring God
Joshua 22—24

Memorize God's Word: Joshua 24:24.

❖ Joshua 22:1-9—Eastern Tribes Return Home

1. Whom did the Reubenites, the Gadites, and the half-tribe of Manasseh obey? How did Joshua describe their obedience and its benefit to others?

   _____

   _____

   _____

2. What could they do now that their service to their brothers had ended?

   _____

   _____

3. Where did they go? What did they take with them?

   _____

   _____

4. What five things did Joshua charge them to do?

   _____

   _____

   _____

   _____

❖ Joshua 22:10-34—The Eastern Tribes' Altar

5. Who built the altar? Where did they build it? What was it like?

_____

_____

6. What did those troubled by this altar say about the altar builders' motives?

_____

_____

7. What did the altar builders say about their motives?

_____

_____

8. What do you think this incident illustrates about how Christians today should settle their differences?

_____

_____

❖ Joshua 23—Joshua's Farewell Message

9. When did Joshua deliver his message?

_____

_____

10. What were Joshua's
    a. reminders? _____

    _____

    b. assurances? _____

    _____

    c. commands? _____

    _____

    d. warnings? _____

    _____

❖ Joshua 24:1-15—A Review of Israel's History

11. How would you outline Joshua's message?

_____

_____

12. What word did Joshua repeat (verses 14-15)?

_____

_____

13. What you think he meant by *"fear"* the Lord?

_____

_____

_____

14. What do you think he meant by *"in sincerity and in faithfulness"*?

_____

_____

_____

❖ Joshua 24:16-33—Joshua's Warning

15. What two attributes of God did Joshua note? What do you think each means?

_____

_____

16. How do these two qualities command a response from God's people? (See Exodus 20:3-5; 1 Peter 1:15-16.)

_____

_____

17. When the Israelites decided to serve the Lord, what warning and guidance did Joshua give?

_____

_____

18. How did the people's two responses differ (verses 18 and 24)?

_____

_____

_____

Apply what you have learned. Joshua exhorted the people to *"be very strong to keep and do"* what God commanded, to *"cling to the LORD your God just as you have done this day,"* and to *"love the LORD your God"* (Joshua 23). He also encouraged them to choose the right way, though they had already chosen wrongly (24:23). Crossing the Jordan into the Promised Land doesn't mean we have arrived, and falling in failure doesn't mean we have to stay down. Whether your current position is high or low, the next movement can always be forward and upward. (See also Philippians 3:12-14; Hosea 6:1-3.) If you have just celebrated a spiritual victory, ask God how you should continue in the same direction. If you have stepped aside from following God, ask God what next step will bring you back.

Joshua: Loving and Honoring God
Joshua 22—24

Sending the Eastern Tribes Home

Conquering the Promised Land took about seven years. In that time, *"not one word of all the good promises that the* LORD *had made to the house of Israel had failed"* (21:45). Joshua sent the soldiers from the eastern tribes home with enemy plunder to share with their families. He praised them and said they must love the Lord their God, walk in His ways, keep His commandments, cling to Him, and serve Him with all their heart and soul (22:5).

The homebound tribes built a large altar near the Jordan River in Canaan. The western tribes assumed the worst—that this altar meant rebellion against God—and planned war against their brothers. Because they had been punished earlier for the sin of a few, they were afraid and now wanted to obey God fully. Aaron's grandson Phineas and a chief from each tribe asked the two-and-a-half tribes to explain; they said the altar was not for burnt offerings but for a witness to future generations that both eastern and western tribes were united as Israelites.

Think about the relationship lessons we can learn from these two groups of Israelites. From the western tribes we learn not to assume the motives behind others' actions. They made false assumptions about the altar's purpose and prepared for war! From the eastern tribes we learn how to answer those who accuse us falsely. They appealed to God. They lovingly explained their motives; the altar was a witness of a reunited people under God. Misunderstandings happen when we judge others without knowing their intentions. God alone knows the heart. Only as we seek to understand others' motives and communicate with them in love will we find genuine unity.

Joshua's Farewell Address

Though the conquest was mostly complete, the occupation was incomplete; the Israelites disobeyed God's command to drive out the Canaanites. As God predicted, the Canaanites were thorns in their sides and barbs in their eyes (Numbers 33:55). Knowing he would soon die, Joshua reminded the Israelites of all God had done for them. He admonished, *"Be very strong to keep and to do all that is written in the Book of the Law of Moses* [the Pentateuch], *turning aside from it neither to the right hand nor to the left ... but you shall cling to the* LORD *your God just as you have done to this day"* (23:6-8).

The word *"cling"* comes from the Hebrew word *dabahk, to be glued.* Like them, we must "glue" ourselves to God. Joshua then warned, as did Moses before he died, *"Be very careful, therefore, to love the* LORD *your God. For if you turn back and cling to the remnant of these nations remaining among you ... know for certain that the* LORD *your God will no longer drive out these nations before you, but they shall be a snare and a trap for you, a whip on your sides and thorns in your eyes, until you perish from off this good ground that the* LORD *your God has given you"* (23:11-13). Disobedience not only prevents victory but brings a curse. While Joshua reminded them of God's faithfulness, he also warned that rejecting God would result in sorrow and death.

Congregating at Shechem

Because of temptations on all sides to worship other gods, we also should heed Joshua's warnings. Joshua again reminded the Israelites what God had done for them. God placed this remembering pattern throughout His Word; more than three-fourths of the Bible concerns God's involvement in human history! For example, John concluded his gospel: *"Jesus did many other signs in the presence of the disciples, which are not written in this book; but these are written so that you may believe that Jesus is the Christ, the Son of God, and that by believing you may have life in His name"* (20:30-31). Even the Ten Commandments have a personal and historical prologue: *"I am the* LORD *your God, who brought you out of the land of Egypt, out of the house of slavery*" (Deuteronomy 5:6).

God's gracious, mighty intervention for His people preceded almost all His commandments. Joshua understood this very well. Thus, before giving God's mandate to the Israelite leaders, he passionately told about God's great deeds in the past. Then he commanded them to *"Put away the gods that your fathers served beyond the River and in Egypt, and serve the LORD"* (24:14) and solemnly challenged them to *"choose this day whom you will serve ... But as for me and my house, we will serve the LORD"* (24:15). They replied that they will not *"forsake the LORD to serve other gods"* (24:16), but will indeed *"serve the LORD"* (24:21). Joshua gave them a choice to believe or to reject, to follow or to disobey. God gives all people the same choice today.

Two significant results came out of this gathering: (1) Joshua and the people established a new pact with God—*"Joshua made a covenant with the people that day"* and (2) *"put in place statutes and rules for them at Shechem"* (24:25). Repeating a covenant may help all those who tend to forget. Joshua recorded the words in the Book of the Law of God, which probably refers to the book of Joshua.

Because the closing passage refers to Joshua's death, another writer must also have contributed to this book, but we do know that Joshua wrote most of it. The gathering at Shechem must have been one of the most unforgettable moments for the people of Joshua's time. In response to a vivid and moving challenge, they pledged to serve only the Lord. These Israelites served the Lord faithfully while under Joshua's and the elders' leadership. After these leaders died, the people were not so faithful. How wonderful that our Joshua—our Savior Jesus—is ever alive, so that we need not fail as we look to Him, *"the founder and perfecter of our faith"* (Hebrews 12:2).

Personalize this lesson.

✓ When you think in terms of a personal and intimate relationship between you and God, consider what His jealousy reveals about His love for you. If God is jealous for you, how does that make you want to respond to Him? How does God's jealousy make you feel about the idols in your life? Ponder these things as you meditate on what Jesus said is the greatest commandment: *"You shall love the Lord your God with all your heart and with all your soul and with all your mind"* (Matthew 22:37).

Lesson 8

Judges: God's Chosen Deliverers
Judges 1—3

Memorize God's Word: Psalm 22:28.

❖ Judges 1:1-15—Israel Fights the Remaining Canaanites

1. After Joshua died, what did the Israelites ask God? What was God's answer?

   _____

   _____

2. From the events in verses 1-4, what do you learn about God and His character?

   _____

   _____

   _____

3. Scan Judges 1:16-36. What phrase is repeated several times?

   _____

   _____

   _____

4. How did this affect Israel's relationship with God? (See also Joshua 23.)

   _____

   _____

   _____

❖ Judges 2:1-10—Israel Fails to Keep God's Covenant

5. How had God been faithful to the Israelites?

    _____

    _____

6. How had the Israelites been unfaithful to God? What were the consequences?

    _____

    _____

7. What was the Israelites' response to the angel's pronouncement?

    _____

    _____

8. What was true about Joshua and the generation who served the Lord (2:7)?

    _____

    _____

9. What was true about the generation after them (2:10)?

    _____

    _____

❖ Judges 2:11-23—God Raises up Judges to Deliver Israel

10. What angered God so much that He gave the Israelites over to plunderers (2:11-14)?

    _____

    _____

11. Whom did the Lord raise up to save the Israelites from their plunderers? Why?

    _____

    _____

12. What happened within Israel when a judge died? What made God angry with Israel again (verse 20)?

_____

_____

_____

13. Why didn't God drive out the nations Joshua left unconquered?

_____

_____

_____

❖ Judges 3:1-11—Israel Tested by War

14. God tested Israel to see if they would obey His commands (3:4). What actions showed whether they did or didn't pass this test?

_____

_____

_____

15. What resulted from their actions? What did they do then?

_____

_____

_____

16. Whom did the Lord send to deliver them? Why was he successful?

_____

_____

_____

❖ Judges 3:12-31—God's Judges Deliver His People

17. What cycle repeated with each judge?

_____

18. What does this teach you about God?

_____

_____

_____

_____

Apply what you have learned. When the angel of the Lord pronounced God's judgment for Israel's disobedience, the people *"lifted up their voices and wept"* (See 2:1-5.) Knowledge of their sin grieved them. When God makes us aware of our sin, it is an act of grace—a chance to repent and receive God's promised forgiveness. (See 2 Corinthians 7:10; 1 John 1:9.) When Nathan confronted David for adultery and murder, David repented on the spot (2 Samuel 12:13). When another prophet called Ahab on his sin, Ahab went home *"vexed and sullen"* (1 Kings 20:43). God may send you someone who cares enough to confront you about a sin in your life. When that happens, let the sorrow that leads to repentance be your response.

Judges: God's Chosen Deliverers
Judges 1—3

Introduction

The Israelites neglected God's command to expel all the Canaanites from their land. As a result, they often succumbed to the Canaanites' pagan culture and idolatry. Then a pattern began: they crumbled spiritually and morally, and neighboring nations defeated them. Then, humiliated and oppressed, they groaned to God for deliverance, and God raised up leaders (judges) to save them. But as soon as these judges died, the Israelites sinned again. The book of Judges is cyclical: Israel's sin caused suffering that brought repentance that resulted in salvation. For an overview of events recorded in the book of Judges, see the chart in the Appendix on page 105.

The title *Judges* in Hebrew is *Shophetim,* but the verb *to judge* comes from the Hebrew word *shaphat, to defend, deliver, govern.* The Hebrew judges delivered Israel from her enemies and administered God's commands.

Not all of Israel's judges were national leaders. Some (Shamgar, Tola, Jair, Ibzan, Elon, and Abdon) were local chieftains who concurrently ruled in their respective districts. Israel's judges were like Rome's consuls in Jesus' day. The Hebrew *shophetim,* though, were leaders endowed with God's wisdom and power, chosen and called by God. Like Joshua, most of them were military leaders. Some, such as Deborah, were prophets and nonmilitary people.

The time from Abraham through the judges was an era of theocracy; God Himself was King. People like Moses, Joshua, and the judges were God's agents, regents of the invisible King. Sadly, the Israelites did not cherish God's sovereign rule. Judges 17:6 and 21:25 describe Israel's moral and spiritual character: *"In those days there was no king in Israel.*

Everyone did what was right in his own eyes" (17:6; 21:25). In His mercy, God raised up judges to lead the people back to Himself. They taught the Israelites to fear and obey God.

The era of the judges lasted from Joshua's death until Saul became Israel's first king, a period of several centuries. The prophet Samuel—who lived between the period of the judges and that of the kings—probably wrote this book, which can be divided into the last days of Joshua (1:1–2:5); the judges of Israel (2:6–16:31); and other events (17:1–21:25).

Caleb and Othniel

Caleb was consistently confident about the conquest of the Promised Land (Numbers 14:9; Judges 1:12). After godly Caleb came courageous Othniel. The name *Othniel* means *God is might.*

Othniel did not take part in Baal worship but stayed faithful to God. Being of Caleb's household (his father was Caleb's brother, and he married Caleb's daughter), he surely experienced God's faithfulness and power. He was a man of the Spirit: *"The Spirit of the Lord was upon him, and he judged Israel"* (3:10). Previous Scriptures point out other leaders endowed with God's Holy Spirit, leaders like Joseph, the 70 elders assisting Moses, and Joshua. The same message resounds throughout Scripture: *"'Not by might, nor by power, but by My Spirit,' says the Lord of hosts"* (Zechariah 4:6). That same Holy Spirit is available to Christians today (see John 14:16-17).

The Israelites *"did what was evil in the sight of the LORD,"* forgetting God and serving the Baals and Asheroth (3:7). Because of this disobedience to God's commands, God allowed the Mesopotamian king to attack and abuse them. They were slaves for eight years. Like their ancestors, this generation cried out to God for mercy and deliverance.

The Lord heard their plea and called Othniel to deliver Israel from these enemies. With God's help, Othniel accomplished his mission. The nation rested from foreign tyranny for 40 years. But soon after Othniel's death, the Israelites again *"did what was evil in the sight of the LORD"* (3:12).

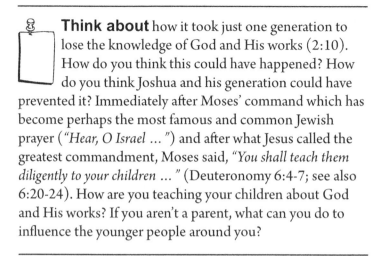

Think about how it took just one generation to lose the knowledge of God and His works (2:10). How do you think this could have happened? How do you think Joshua and his generation could have prevented it? Immediately after Moses' command which has become perhaps the most famous and common Jewish prayer (*"Hear, O Israel ... "*) and after what Jesus called the greatest commandment, Moses said, *"You shall teach them diligently to your children ... "* (Deuteronomy 6:4-7; see also 6:20-24). How are you teaching your children about God and His works? If you aren't a parent, what can you do to influence the younger people around you?

Ehud and Shamgar

The result of their sin was disastrous. God allowed Eglon, king of Moab, to capture Jericho and control it for 18 years. The Israelites again became slaves and begged God for help. In His mercy, He raised up Ehud to confront King Eglon.

An interesting fact about Ehud was his left-handedness. In biblical culture, no one ever used his left hand to pass anything to another person. To use one's left hand in public was considered bad manners. Scripture consistently refers to the "right hand" as a symbol of honor (Mark 12:36; Revelation 1:16-17). Yet God chose and called Ehud because He knew his heart. And with his left hand, Ehud defeated King Eglon.

All the way, Ehud recognized God's power and presence in Israel's victory. He trusted in the almighty God even before the actual battle and told all Israel to follow him, because God had already given them the victory over the Moabites (3:28). When the Israelites acted on Ehud's statement of faith, they witnessed an amazing victory over Eglon's powerful army. The people of Israel then enjoyed peace and rest in their land for 80 years—possible only because of God's mercy. Though the Israelites often failed Him, He could not forget them (Psalm 89:31-33).

Shamgar followed Ehud, killing 600 Philistines with an oxgoad and saving Israel (3:31).

Personalize this lesson.

✓ Consider the cyclical pattern of Israel's history during the time of the Judges—the people sin, oppression comes, the people desperately cry out to God, God mercifully delivers, the people again sin. Focus on the part about God's merciful deliverance and meditate on its repetition: God showed mercy ... and again showed mercy ... and again, and again. Our sin and hard times happen over and over, but His mercies do, too. They are new every morning. (See Lamentations 3:22-23.) If you find yourself spinning in a cycle like the Israelites, let God's relentless mercy stand out to you. With His great love as your motivation, you can break out of that cycle into a new pattern of loving, obeying, and abiding in God. Where have you seen God's love for you lately? How can you respond to His mercy?

Deborah and Barak
Judges 4—5

Memorize God's Word: Judges 5:3.

❖ Judges 4:1-5—History Repeats Itself

1. What are the main events in verses 1-3?

    _____

    _____

    _____

2. How did Israel know not to do *"evil in the sight of the* LORD*"* by serving idols? (See Judges 3:7; Exodus 20:3-6.)

    _____

    _____

    _____

3. What does God desire from His people? (See Matthew 22:36-38.)

    _____

    _____

    _____

4. What were Deborah's two roles in serving Israel? (If you wish, use a dictionary to define them.)

    _____

    _____

    _____

❖ Judges 4:6-13—God Uses Deborah and Barak to Deliver Israel

5. Who, according to Deborah, commanded Barak? What were the commands?

    _____

    _____

6. Why did Deborah accompany Barak on his military mission?

    _____

    _____

7. What facts do you observe about Barak? What is your opinion of him?

    _____

    _____

    _____

8. Have you ever been afraid to obey God's commands? What might help you be strong and courageous to take the next step of obedience?

    _____

    _____

    _____

9. When he heard Barak had gathered an army at Mount Tabor, how did Sisera respond?

    _____

    _____

    _____

❖ Judges 4:14-24—Sisera's Defeat

10. How did Deborah inspire Barak?

    _____

    _____

11. Compare Hebrews 11:1 to Deborah's words to Barak. What was
    her faith like?

    _____

    _____

    _____

12. What happened in the battle?

    _____

    _____

    _____

13. To where did Sisera flee? Why?

    _____

    _____

14. What happened to Sisera? What did Deborah prophesy about
    him earlier?

    _____

    _____

    _____

❖ Judges 5—Deborah's Song of Victory

15. Who sang the song, and to whom? What were the people's
    inspired responses?

    _____

    _____

    _____

16. What parts of the song revealed Israel's desperate condition?

    _____

    _____

    _____

    _____

17. What battle details did you learn from the song that you didn't
    know from chapter 4?

_____

_____

_____

_____

_____

18. How did God respond to the Israelites' seasons of strength and
    weakness? How could this encourage you?

_____

_____

_____

_____

Apply what you have learned. If you were
to write a worship song, what details would you
include? What would the song reveal about your
circumstances, what God has done in your life, or your
relationship with Him? Could you write one and share it
with someone?

Deborah and Barak
Judges 4—5

Slipping Back Into Sin

God chose Israel to be His holy people. From them He would bring forth the Savior of the world. But idols seduced them, and they often forgot their God. When Moses was slow in coming down from Sinai, they asked Aaron to make a golden calf and worshiped it. As punishment, 3,000 people died that same day (Exodus 32:1-6, 25-29). God's Law explained such severe retribution: *"Take care, lest you forget the covenant of the LORD your God … For the LORD is a consuming fire, a jealous God"* (Deuteronomy 4:23-24). Several phrases in Judges describe God correcting His people: *"The LORD … gave them over to plunderers, who plundered them. And He sold them into the hand of their surrounding enemies"* (Judges 2:14); *"to test Israel"* (3:1); *"the LORD sold them into the hand of Jabin king of Canaan"* (4:2). God's discipline was severe and painful, but also righteous, just, and motivated by love. (See Hebrews 12:5-11; Proverbs 3:11-12.)

Before Moses died, he described the curses that would come if the people disobeyed God: *"The LORD will cause you to be defeated before your enemies … you shall be a horror to all the kingdoms of the earth. … You shall betroth a wife, but another man shall ravish her. … Your sons and your daughters shall be given to another people, while your eyes look on and fail with longing for them all day long … you shall be only oppressed and crushed continually, so that you will be driven mad by the sights that your eyes see."* (See Deuteronomy 28:15-68.) Imagine two decades of such oppression. No wonder they cried to the Lord for help (Judges 4:3)!

Deborah: Prophetess and Deliverer

Unlike the previous judges, Deborah was a prophetess. Far from discriminating against women, God used female prophets throughout history, including Miriam, Aaron's sister (Exodus 15:20); Deborah, one of Israel's deliverers (Judges 4:4); Huldah (2 Kings 22:14); Noadiah (Nehemiah 6:14); Isaiah's wife (Isaiah 8:3); Elizabeth, mother of John the Baptist (Luke 1:41-45); Anna, a widow (Luke 2:36-38); and the daughters of Philip the evangelist (Acts 21:9).

Deborah judged under a palm tree planted between Ramah (*height* in Hebrew) and Bethel. Many towns and cities built on hilltops were known as Ramah. Bethel means *house of God* and received its name from Jacob when he dreamed of angels ascending and descending a ladder from heaven (Genesis 28:10-22).

Deborah showed her confidence in God and His word, accepted His promise as if it had already happened, and was willing to let God choose someone else to carry out the action and receive the credit. Deborah was so close to God that Barak depended on her and insisted she join him in battle.

Deborah was one of many devout women chosen by God for His people's welfare. Hannah begged God for a child and gave her son Samuel to the Lord (1 Samuel 1:10-20, 27-28). Ruth the Moabite chose to align herself with God's people (Ruth 1:16-17) and became ancestress to David and Jesus. Mary placed herself in God's hands (Luke 1:38) and brought our Savior into the world. Timothy's grandmother, Lois, and his mother, Eunice, lived a life of faith and influenced Timothy's faith (2 Timothy 1:5). Society today seeks to elevate women's roles, but God has elevated them all along.

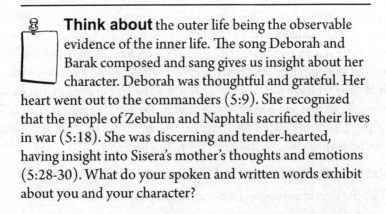

Think about the outer life being the observable evidence of the inner life. The song Deborah and Barak composed and sang gives us insight about her character. Deborah was thoughtful and grateful. Her heart went out to the commanders (5:9). She recognized that the people of Zebulun and Naphtali sacrificed their lives in war (5:18). She was discerning and tender-hearted, having insight into Sisera's mother's thoughts and emotions (5:28-30). What do your spoken and written words exhibit about you and your character?

Barak: Commander of Israel

Deborah wanted a military leader to liberate Israel from Jabin, king of the northern Canaanites. She summoned Barak, son of Abinoam from Kedesh-naphtali. But Barak lacked Deborah's confidence. He needed encouragement and told her candidly, *"If you will go with me, I will go, but if you will not go with me, I will not go"* (4:8). Barak was perhaps the only commander directed and supported by a woman. Deborah went with him to station his army at Mount Tabor (4:10, 14). Barak obeyed Deborah totally, realizing that the people looked to Deborah as their leader. With her at his side, they rallied to the battle.

Think about Barak needing someone to further his faith in God. Many believers today need other Christians to inspire them and build up their faith. Others are like Deborah—able to trust God and His word. Perhaps most often, each person has been a little like both. When we are like Deborah, let us build up and strengthen others. But when we are weak, let us humbly accept support that we may have victory over unbelief, as did Barak.

Deborah and Barak's song reveals details not mentioned in chapter 4. It emphasizes that the Israelites willingly offered themselves to fight the Canaanites (5:2). It tells which tribes responded to Barak's appeal and which ones *"sat still"* (5:13-18). It records the exact place of battle (5:19) and how the Lord used rain and flood to confound the enemies (5:20-22). It imagines Sisera's mother's restlessness as she waited for her son's return (5:28). And it describes the ruthlessness of Canaanite soldiers who would molest the girls of occupied lands (5:30).

After Deborah and Barak gained victory through God's power, they offered Him a praise song. They glorified the One who had so wonderfully answered His people's cry and delivered them from oppression. They worshiped *"the God of Israel"* (5:3) who loved and cared for His people.

Personalize this lesson.

☑ God's design is that His people build one another up. Every Christian needs other Christians. God used Deborah to bolster Barak's faith in Him. God does the same today by encouraging you to help someone else or sending someone to help you. When you realize you can help a fellow believer grow in faith, you recognize and participate in God's design. Perhaps you could ask God if He has a specific relationship in mind for you to give more of yourself to. Or perhaps you are on the receiving side. It may feel easier or more comfortable to give than to receive, but don't let pride keep you from accepting another's help. Jesus may have sent that person to help you! Jesus said if we won't receive from Him we can't be a part of what He's doing. (See John 13:8.) If someone needs your service, pick up the towel and basin of water. And if yours are the dirty feet, go ahead and take the washing.

Gideon: Mighty Warrior
Judges 6—8

❖ **Judges 6:1-16—God Calls Gideon**

1. Why did the Lord hand the Israelites over to the Midianites? (See also Judges 2:11-15.)

   _____

   _____

   _____

2. What strategy did the Midianites use to subdue the land?

   _____

   _____

   _____

3. What was the prophet's message? Why do you think God sent a prophet before sending a deliverer?

   _____

   _____

   _____

   _____

4. What was Gideon doing when the *"angel of the LORD"* came? How did the angel address him?

   _____

   _____

   _____

5. What did Gideon ask? How did the angel reply?

_____

_____

❖ Judges 6:17-32—Gideon Obeys God

6. How did Gideon discover that his visitor was truly the angel of the LORD?

_____

_____

7. What did God ask Gideon to do before delivering Israel?

_____

_____

8. Why do you think he needed to do this first?

_____

_____

9. What did you learn about the townspeople?

_____

_____

10. What did you learn about Joash, Gideon's father?

_____

_____

❖ Judges 6:33–7:8—Gideon Seeks Reassurance

11. How did God empower Gideon to lead His people?

_____

_____

12. What did Gideon ask of God? Why?

_____

_____

13. Why did God reduce Gideon's army?

_____

_____

14. From verses 3 and 5, why do you think God used this criteria for reducing the troops?

_____

_____

❖ Judges 7:9-25—Unconventional Warfare Brings Victory

15. How did God give Gideon extra assurance?

_____

_____

16. How did Gideon respond to this encouragement?

_____

_____

17. What instructions did Gideon give to his men? What were they to use as weapons?

_____

_____

❖ Judges 8—An Insidious Enemy

18. What did the Israelites propose to Gideon because of his victory?

_____

_____

_____

19. Why did he refuse their offer?

_____

_____

20. What did Gideon do instead? What were the results?

_____

_____

_____

21. What adjectives would describe Gideon's character?

_____

_____

_____

_____

Apply what you have learned. Though God already gave Gideon repeated assurances of victory, He considered Gideon's fear and encouraged him yet again: *"I have given* [the Midianite camp] *into your hand. But if you are afraid ... "* (7:9). What a demonstration of sensitivity to Gideon's heart and emotions! Gideon's on-the-spot response: worship. Then he returned to his own camp, commanded his men, and defeated the Midianites. God intimately cares for you, too, and offers repeated assurances in His Word. Whenever you read a promise, encouragement, or assurance in the Bible, respond like Gideon. Worship God, encourage others, and move forward to the next task God wants you to accomplish for Him.

Gideon: Mighty Warrior
Judges 6—8

After Deborah and Barak led the Israelites through 40 years of peace, the people again forgot God and sinned. Therefore God tested them using surrounding nations—the Midianites and Amalekites (6:1-6). The Midianites, a nomadic tribe, shared blood ties with Israel through Abraham and Keturah (Genesis 25:1-2). This tribe so ravaged Israel that they *"cried out for help"* to the Lord—a frequently recurring Old Testament phrase (see Exodus 2:23). It was a repentant cry, and God responded positively.

The Call of Gideon

Whenever the Israelites returned to God in repentance, He lovingly received them. This time, God sent His angel to set apart a young man from the tribe of Manasseh—Gideon, the son of Joash. When God called him, Gideon was threshing wheat in a hot, dusty winepress instead of outdoors, for fear of the Midianites. The angel of the LORD called Gideon a *"mighty man of valor,"* and he responded, *"if the LORD is with us, why then has all this happened to us?"* (6:13). God already answered that question, telling the Israelites they had not listened to His voice.

Strong in God's power, Gideon was to *"save Israel from the hand of Midian"* (6:14). He replied, *"Please, Lord, how can I save Israel? Behold, my clan is the weakest in Manasseh, and I am the least in my father's house"* (6:15). Throughout history, God chose those who felt inadequate to be His leaders. When God called Moses, he responded in the same way: *"Who am I ... Please send someone else"* (Exodus 3:11; 4:13). Isaiah cried, *"Woe is me! ... for I am a man of unclean lips"* (Isaiah 6:5). Jeremiah could not see himself as God's spokesman: *"I do not know how to speak"* (Jeremiah 1:6). Paul said, *"For I am the least of the apostles, unworthy to be called an apostle"* (1 Corinthians 15:9).

God delights in the one who responds as Isaiah did after confessing his inability: *"Here I am. Send me!"* (Isaiah 6:8). When we say yes to God, He assures us of His presence: *"I will be with you"* (Judges 6:16). When the Lord is with us, who else do we need?

The night the angel of the LORD visited Gideon, he bravely followed God's instructions to destroy the altar of Baal and the Asherah pole. It is crucial to remove everything spiritually and morally devastating to Israel. Gideon risked his life by obeying God; the men of the town demanded his life (6:30). When Joash defended his son, not one man dared touch Gideon. They renamed him Jerubbaal, meaning *"let Baal contend against him"* (6:31-32).

The Midianites, Amalekites, and eastern tribes heard of the incident and strategized to attack Gideon and Israel. The battle was not Gideon's: the Spirit of God now filled him, and he sounded the trumpet call to battle. But he wanted still another sign from God that would reassure him of victory. Their situation seemed hopeless: a few brave farmers with homemade weapons against a mighty force (*"like locusts in number"*) with countless camels. God answered Gideon, first with a soaking wet fleece on dry ground, then with a dry fleece on ground wet with morning dew, just as Gideon requested.

Think about how Gideon laid a fleece to confirm God's will for him. He was ready to perform his dangerous task if he were sure God had called him. God honored his requests, because He wanted Gideon to be sure of His will for him. Let us offer ourselves fully to God, allow Him to transform us, order our lives according to His will, and obey Him fully as did Gideon (Romans 12:1-2).

The Victorious Battle

Gideon called up brave men from Manasseh, Asher, Zebulun, and Naphtali. About 32,000 responded—not many against an army perhaps six times that size. But God reduced the Israelite manpower, sending 22,000 home and saying that still too many remained. Israel might *"boast over Me, saying, 'My own hand has saved me'"* (7:2). He told Gideon to screen the remaining men; only 300 met the Lord's requirements. Now God was ready to lead them to victory. It was vital that the Israelites knew it was God—not their military might—that won the battle. Victories come *"not by might nor, by power, but by* [God's] *Spirit"* (Zechariah 4:6). God used a dream to paralyze the Midianites' hearts with fear and to encourage Gideon and his 300 men. They followed His orders through to a victory of faith more than equal to the victory at Jericho. Without doubt, it was the Lord who fought on behalf of Israel. *"A sword for the* LORD *and for Gideon!"* (7:20).

Criticism, Rejection, Temptation

Instead of greeting Gideon with joy after his victory, the Ephraimites chided him. They felt slighted because they were called in at the last. Gideon wisely defused their anger by doing as Proverbs 15:1 suggests: *"A soft answer turns away wrath."* But he dealt firmly with the men of Succoth and Penuel when they refused supplies for his men. Gideon and his band of 300 men pursued the eastern invaders into the desert and defeated all 15,000 of them on their own ground. Hot, tired, hungry, they fought valiantly because God was with them.

Having watched their enemies' downfall, and now having freedom and peace, the Israelites asked Gideon to be their king. He nobly declined. But then he erred greatly by asking for their plunder of gold earrings and making it into an ephod. This ephod is unlike the priestly ephod (Exodus 39:2-5). Israel worshiped it as an idol, *"and it became a snare to Gideon and to his family"* (Judges 8:27). The worship of this ephod eventually led to the return of Baal-worship. That did not occur until after Gideon's death when the Israelites *"turned again and whored after the Baals"* (8:33). However, the land rested from war for 40 years—the rest of Gideon's life. We can see in Gideon's story the marvelous results of God working through just one man.

Personalize this lesson.

✓ Gideon's story shows us that the weak and inadequate may be God's perfect choice for a mission. Perhaps God gave you a task precisely because you're inadequate for it! The apostle Paul said he was unfit to be the apostle he already was: *"unworthy to be called an apostle … but by the grace of God I am what I am"* (1 Corinthians 15:9-10). Counterintuitively, Paul's realization that he was inadequate for the task is what strengthened him for the task: *"and His grace toward me was not in vain. On the contrary, I worked harder than any of them, though it was not I, but the grace of God that is with me"* (1 Corinthians 15:10). Think of the different tasks or roles God is calling you to at this point in your life. Do you feel unfit for any of them? How can you take your doubts and fears to God and move forward in this task? Perhaps what God wants from you is not so much ability but willingness to trust Him.

Jephthah: the Judge
Judges 9—12

❖ Judges 9—Abimelech Rules Over Shechem

1. How did Abimelech become king in Shechem?

2. How would you summarize Jotham's parable (verses 8-15)?

3. What was Jotham's curse?

4. How was the curse fulfilled?

❖ Judges 10:1-9; Psalm 106:34-43—Israelites Suffer Sin's Consequences

5. What words and phrases describe the Israelites' suffering because of their sin?

_____

_____

_____

6. According to Psalm 106, what did the Israelites do to make themselves vulnerable to sin?

_____

_____

7. In Psalm 106, how did God react to their sin?

_____

_____

❖ Judges 10:10-16; Psalm 106:44-45—Israel Again Cries to God for Help

8. Considering each part of Israel's appeal, what was their attitude toward God (Judges 10:15-16)?

_____

_____

_____

9. From Psalm 106:44-45, what do you learn about God?

_____

_____

_____

10. Which words from these two verses have special meaning for you? Why?

_____

_____

❖ Judges 11:1-33—Israel Calls on Jephthah

11. From verses 1-3, what do you learn about Jephthah?

_____

_____

_____

12. What did the elders of Gilead ask Jephthah to do? Why do you think they asked this of him?

_____

_____

_____

13. What was the Ammonite king's reason for attacking Israel? What was Jephthah's response?

_____

_____

_____

_____

14. How did Jephthah win the battle?

_____

_____

_____

❖ Judges 11:34–12:15—Jephthah's Vow

15. What guidelines do the following verses give about vows?

    a.   Deuteronomy 23:21-23 _____

_____

_____

    b. Matthew 5:33-37 _____

_____

_____

16. What was Jephthah's vow?

_____

_____

_____

17. Why do you think Jephthah felt he couldn't take back his vow?

_____

_____

_____

Apply what you have learned. If God has convicted you of a sin, perhaps the five phrases in Judges 10:15-16 could guide your repentance and response: (1) *"We have sinned."* Confess your sin. (2) *"Do to us whatever seems good to you."* Surrender yourself to God's judgment and care. He is always good. (See also 2 Samuel 24:14.) (3) *"Only please deliver us this day."* Keep asking for God's deliverance and mercy. (4) *"So they put away the foreign gods from among them."* Change the pattern of the sin. Turn away from the sin and remove it. (5) *"And served the Lord."* While you turn from what *not* to do, also focus on what you *should* do. Ask God how He would like you to serve Him after this repentance.

Jephthah: the Judge
Judges 9—12

After Gideon's death, the Israelites didn't drift into apostasy and sin—
they leaped into it. *"As soon as Gideon died, the people of Israel turned
again and whored after the Baals and made Baal-berith their god"* (8:33).
Gideon himself precipitated their downfall when he made the golden
ephod in Ophrah.

Abimelech

Abimelech governed Israel for three years but was not considered a
judge by biblical writers. His rule was chaotic, marked by a bloody civil
war that ended in his death. The last words of chapter 9 summarize
this period in Jewish history: *"God also made all the evil of the men of
Shechem return on their heads, and upon them came the curse of Jotham
the son of Jerubbaal"* (9:57). After that, Tola, from the tribe of Issachar,
led Israel for 23 years. Jair followed, leading for 22 years. His 30 sons
rode 30 donkeys and controlled 30 cities, indicating wealth and power.
Like Samuel, Tola and Jair were inter-tribal arbitrators or circuit judges
(1 Samuel 7:15-17).

"The people of Israel again did what was evil in the sight of the LORD" (10:6)
by worshiping false gods: Baals; Ashtaroth; gods of Aram, Sidon, Moab;
Molech, god of the Ammonites; and gods of Philistia—Dagon and
Baal-zebub. God then used seven nations to punish Israel. God used the
Ammonites and Philistines to chasten her for lusting after heathen gods
and forsaking her God. In distress, Israel appealed to God. He reminded
her of His past faithfulness in delivering her from many nations and
said, *"Go and cry out to the gods whom you have chosen; let them save you"*
(10:14). Although Israel turned to other gods, she knew help came only
from the one true God.

The nation confessed their sin to God, saying, *"Do to us whatever seems good to You"* (10:15). Israel knew what they needed to do: *"They put away the foreign gods from among them and served the LORD"* (10:16). When they showed their sincerity with right action, God acted on their behalf, even though He knew they would soon fail Him again. God knows each sin we have committed. The sooner we confess it to Him, the sooner He will forgive and cleanse us (1 John 1:9).

Think about how the Israelites sinned profoundly, yet God always helped when they turned to Him in distress. He helps us, too, in our failures and hard times. He walked this earth as a man, experiencing the same temptations and trials we face. He can help us because He did not succumb to them as we often do: *"We do not have a high priest who is unable to sympathize with our weaknesses, but one who ... has been tempted as we are, yet without sin. Let us then with confidence draw near to the throne of grace, that we may receive mercy and find grace to help in time of need"* (Hebrews 4:15-16).

Jephthah

Jephthah, a *"mighty warrior"* (11:1) was the child of a prostitute. His half-brothers drove him away, not wanting to share their inheritance with him. Jephthah fled to Tob, where *"worthless fellows"* followed him—demonstrating the leadership that would one day make Jephthah Israel's national hero.

When Israel grew desperate in the Ammonite war, Gilead's elders went to get Jephthah from the land of Tob. *"Come and be our leader, that we may fight against the Ammonites"* (11:6), they said to the man they had once rejected. Jephthah assumed leadership and showed his knowledge of, and trust in, the God of Abraham, Isaac, and Jacob. The Spirit of the Lord was upon him (11:29).

The rest of chapter 11 records Jephthah's tragic mistake. He vowed that if God gave him victory, *"whatever comes out from the doors of my house to meet me when I return in peace from the Ammonites shall be the LORD's, and I will offer it up for a burnt offering"* (11:31). The one who came out was his daughter—his only child. From the context it appears he offered her as a sacrifice, though it broke his heart (11:35). Human sacrifice was typical of the Canaanite religion, but was abominable to God. He never asks such a thing from us. When Abraham took Isaac to Mount Moriah, God was testing Abraham's attitude toward Him. God kept Abraham from killing Isaac (Genesis 22:1-2, 9-12). Jephthah erred terribly if he vowed human sacrifice to the very God who holds men responsible for taking human life. He could have thrown himself on God's mercy in regard to the broken vow. If he had asked a priest of God, he would have learned that he could redeem his daughter by giving the amount of money stipulated in the Law (Leviticus 27:1-8).

Yet many Bible scholars believe Jephthah's daughter was dedicated as a "living sacrifice," committed in service to God rather than marrying and having children. Several reasons support this stance. Jephthah's daughter asked permission to mourn her virginity, not her death. She and her girlfriends *"went into the hills and wept because she would never marry"* (Judges 11:38, NIV). Nothing in Judges 11 indicates that God condemned Jephthah for this vow. Instead, in the Hebrews "Hall of Faith," Jephthah was recognized alongside Gideon, Barak, Samson, David, Samuel, and the prophets (Hebrews 11:32).

The Ephraimites

The Ephraimites had resented Gideon for excluding them from fighting against Midian (8:1-3). Now, with Jephthah back from war, they threatened to burn down his house. The Ephraimites felt they deserved a place of honor as descendants of Joseph, who was so important in the nation's formative history. They hated to be left out of any event that involved glory and victory. Jephthah made it clear that he had begged for help, but they refused it. Unlike Gideon, he dealt harshly with the Ephraimites, sending 42,000 to their deaths. We cannot begin to understand Jephthah's cruel actions born out of his culture.

Yet Jephthah did lead Israel for six years, and the Spirit of the Lord was upon him. Listed in Hebrews 11 as one who had faith, Jephthah believed in God's promise, and God in His grace empowered him to deliver Israel.

Personalize this lesson.

✓ How much time and thought do you think Jephthah spent on his vow before making it? Jesus is called *"the Word,"* for He manifests to us all that God is (John 1:1, 14). Our word, too, conveys who and what we are, for *"out of the abundance of the heart the mouth speaks"* (Matthew 12:34). Are you currently thinking of making a vow or promise? If so, first meditate on Ecclesiastes 5:2 and Jesus' words in Matthew 5:33-37. After reading the cautions and teachings in these verses, ask God to guide you in any words you speak and any commitments you make.

Samson: the Judge
Judges 13—16

❖ Judges 13:1-7—A Special Visitor

1. A historical cycle surrounded the period of the judges (see Lesson 8 Commentary). What part of that cycle was missing this time? What similarities do you see in our society?

   _____

   _____

   _____

   _____

   _____

2. What do you learn about Manoah's wife (verse 2)? Who told her she would have a baby?

   _____

   _____

   _____

❖ Judges 13:8-25—God's Promise Fulfilled

3. What three things about his son did Manoah ask God to reveal (13:8, 12)?

   _____

   _____

   _____

   _____

4. How did the angel of the LORD answer?

    _____

    _____

5. From verses 24-25, how did God minister to Samson?

    _____

    _____

    _____

❖ Judges 14—Samson Marries a Philistine

6. Why was Samson determined to marry a Philistine?

    _____

    _____

7. What was his parents' response?

    _____

    _____

8. How did God intend to use Samson's marital relationship?

    _____

    _____

9. How did Samson's marriage celebration turn into treachery, murder, and anger?

    _____

    _____

    _____

❖ Judges 15—Samson Slays the Philistines

10. What did Samson do when he found out his wife had been given to another?

    _____

    _____

11. What do verses 9-13 reveal to you about Judah's spiritual condition?

_____

_____

_____

12. When Samson cried out to God (15:18), how did he acknowledge that (a) the victory was God's, and (b) he needed further help?

_____

_____

_____

_____

❖ Judges 16—Samson Falls to Delilah's Wiles

13. From what you have read in this lesson, what do you think was Samson's major weakness?

_____

_____

_____

_____

14. How did Delilah weaken Samson? What brought him to the point of telling her *"all his heart"*?

_____

_____

_____

15. Why did the Philistines gather? What did they do at the gathering?

_____

_____

_____

16. What did Samson ask of God? What happened after he prayed this prayer?

_____

_____

_____

17. In what way is God working through your obedience or failures to accomplish something He desires?

_____

_____

_____

_____

Apply what you have learned. Samson slayed 1,000 Philistines with nothing but a donkey's jawbone—an incredible feat. Immediately after the victory, Samson gave all the credit to God, then realized he was desperately thirsty. He knew he still needed God and cried out for more of His help (Judges 15:18). Victory and total dependence on God go hand in hand. Think back on a spiritual victory you've experienced recently. Thank God that He has accomplished it! After that victory, did you find yourself still needy in a specific area? Acknowledge your dependence on God, and ask for His help.

Samson: the Judge
Judges 13—16

The Philistines

After Jephthah's death, three different judges led Israel. After the third judge died, Israel again did evil in God's sight, and God gave them over to the Philistines for 40 years (13:1).

The Philistines threatened Israel's survival. They occupied a strategic plain along the Mediterranean coast ruling five great strongholds—Ashdod, Gaza, Ashkelon, Gath, and Ekron—and threatened to overrun Israel from the time of Samson through the time of Saul. Besides their key position and numerical power, they controlled the smelting of iron, which allowed them to produce countless military weapons. Israel had none of these advantages (1 Samuel 13:19-22).

Samson's Birth

The Philistines did not oppress Israel as cruelly as other enemies had, but slyly infiltrated the nation by living, trading, and intermarrying with them. They could take over the entire country this way. God used Samson to show Israel that the Philistines must not be tolerated.

An angel of God prophesied Samson's birth to Manoah's barren wife. Manoah asked God how to rear this son, who would be a Nazirite. (The Hebrew word *nazar* means *to be separated from, consecrated unto*.) A Nazirite vow was not always lifelong (note Paul's vow in Acts 18:18), but it was with Samson. A Nazirite was not to touch a corpse, drink wine or alcohol, or cut his hair or beard (Numbers 6:1-21). Sadly, Samson broke each of these vows during his lifetime.

God, who chose Samson from conception, knew his potential to be a good leader. A leader can be a strong force either for good or for destruction. Although Samson was strong physically, he was weak and undisciplined spiritually. What could have been a great story turned out to be a very sad one.

Marriage and Revenge

Samson's destiny and mission were clear: *"The child shall be a Nazirite to God from the womb, and he shall begin to save Israel from the hand of the Philistines"* (13:5). Samson had superhuman strength but had a human nature like ours, confronted with temptations. Through lust he became associated with the *"uncircumcised Philistines"* (14:3) by insisting on marrying a Philistine. Manoah, knowing God forbade intermarriage (Deuteronomy 7:1-6), tried to discourage him. Samson was out of God's will when he married a Philistine. He was stubborn, but God used his marriage to begin to deliver Israel from the Philistines (14:4).

On his way to visit his bride-to-be, Samson encountered a lion. God's Spirit *"rushed upon him,"* and he killed the lion with his bare hands. On his way home, he found a honeycomb in the lion's body. He brought some honey to his parents but didn't tell them about its source, because he violated a vow by touching the carcass. Later, during his seven-day wedding feast where wine flowed freely, Samson posed a riddle attached to a reward or penalty. His guests couldn't solve it and threatened his wife with death if she didn't get the answer from him. The poor bride wept all through the feast until Samson gave in and told her the answer, which she passed on to her people.

In response, Samson struck down 30 men in Ashkelon, took their clothes, and gave them to those who answered the riddle. Enraged, he then returned to his father's house. God gave Samson superhuman strength, even when he acted in anger. God worked to strike down 30 Philistines to start breaking their domination over Israel. When his wife's father gave her to the friend who attended him at the wedding, Samson burned Philistine fields, vineyards, and olive groves with fox tails on fire. They retaliated by burning his wife and father-in-law to death; Samson in turn killed many of them. The unofficial war between them escalated. After killing 1,000 Philistines with a donkey's jawbone, a thirsty Samson prayed for help, and God kindly provided water for him.

Samson's Tragic End

Samson visited a harlot in Gaza, resulting in another bizarre display of strength as he escaped the men lying in wait for him there. He broke out of the city in the middle of the night, tearing loose and carrying the heavy city gates on his shoulders for a 38-mile hike uphill.

Once again, Samson showed weakness in his relationship with a woman. The Philistines used Delilah to do what their mighty armies could not do—capture and defeat Samson. She didn't hide her desire to know the source of Samson's strength in order to subdue him. But he was sure he could deceive her and foolishly kept coming to her after she tried three times to trick and enslave him. Delilah nagged until he gave in, telling her that his strength lay in his unshorn hair.

Samson's downfall began when he violated his Nazarite vow. But his greatest tragedy shows in these words: *"But he did not know that the* Lord *had left him"* (16:20). The Philistines seized him, gouged his eyes out, and took him to prison where he turned a millstone to grind flour. However, his hair started growing back.

Think about how the Spirit of the Lord *"rushed upon"* Samson when he killed the lion, struck down 30 men at Ashkelon, and broke through binding ropes like fire burns through flax. How surprised and bewildered Samson must have been when he realized the Lord had left him (16:20)! But Christians need not fear such devastating abandonment, for we have the New Testament promise that God *"will never leave you nor forsake you"* (Hebrews 13:5).

Meanwhile, the Philistine rulers assembled to rejoice and sacrifice to their god Dagon, saying, *"Our god has given Samson our enemy into our hand"* (16:23). As they brought him into the temple to entertain them, he asked God to avenge him for his eyes. He braced himself against the two main pillars and said, *"Let me die with the Philistines."* (16:30). God gave him a surge of strength and the house fell on the lords and all the Philistines in it. So Samson killed more Philistines at his death than in his life. This strong, complex man led Israel for 20 years.

Personalize this lesson.

✓ The remaining chapters of Judges chronicle Israel's steady walk away from God. Repeatedly in chapters 17-21 we read, *"In those days there was no king in Israel. Everyone did what was right in his own eyes"* (17:6, 21:25). In a quick read of these chapters, you will discover what Israel did that was right in their own eyes. The details are tragic and sobering.

The book of Judges begs an honest reflection on our own decisions. Are there ways that you have decided to live that are "right in your own eyes"? Be courageous and talk with God about those choices. Ask Him if they are right in His eyes, too. Willingly respond to what He shows you. This kind of authenticity with God will lead you in a steady walk with Him rather than away from Him.

Oppressors	Duration	Judges	Duration	Texts
Mesopotamians	8 years	Othniel	40 years	3:7-11
Moabites	18 years	Ehud Shamgar	80 years	3:12-31
Canaanites	20 years	Deborah Barak	40 years	4—5
Midianites	7 years	Gideon	40 years	6—8
Abimelech	3 years	Tola Jair	23 years 22 years	9:1-10:3
Ammonites	18 years	Jephthah Ibzan Elon Abdon	6 years 7 years 10 years 8 years	10:6-12:7 12:8-10 12:11-12 12:13-15
Philistines	40 years	Samson	20 years	12—16

Small Group Leader's Guide

While *Engaging God's Word* is great for personal study, it is generally even more effective and enjoyable when studied with others. Studying with others provides different perspectives and insights, care, prayer support, and fellowship that studying on your own does not. Depending on your personal circumstances, consider studying with your family or spouse, with a friend, in a Sunday school, with a small group at church, work, or in your neighborhood, or in a mentoring relationship.

In a traditional Community Bible Study class, your study would involve a proven four-step method: personal study, a small group discussion facilitated by a trained leader, a lecture covering the passage of Scripture, and a written commentary about the same passage. *Engaging God's Word* provides two of these four steps with the study questions and commentary. When you study with a group, you add another of these—the group discussion. And if you enjoy teaching, you could even provide a modified form of the fourth, the lecture, which in a small group setting might be better termed a wrap-up talk.

Here are some suggestions to help leaders facilitate a successful group study.

1. Decide how long you would like each group meeting to last. For a very basic study, without teaching, time for fellowship, or group prayer, plan on one hour. If you want to allow for fellowship before the meeting starts, add at least 15 minutes. If you plan to give a short teaching, add 15 or 20 minutes. If you also want time for group prayer, add another 10 or 15 minutes. Depending on the components you include for your group, each session will generally last between one and two hours.

2. Set a regular time and place to meet. Meeting in a church classroom or a conference room at work is fine. Meeting in a home is also a good option, and sometimes more relaxed and comfortable.

3. Publicize the study and/or personally invite people to join you.

4. Begin praying for those who have committed to come. Continue to pray for them individually throughout the course of the study.

5. Make sure everyone has his or her own book at least a week before you meet for the first time.

6. Encourage group members to read the first lesson and do the questions before they come to the group meeting.

7. Prepare your own lesson.

8. Prepare your wrap-up talk, if you plan to give one. Here is a simple process for developing a wrap-up talk:

    a.   Divide the passage you are studying into two or three divisions. Jot down the verses for each division and describe the content of each with one complete sentence that answers the question, "What is the passage about?"

    b.   Decide on the central idea of your wrap-up talk. The central idea is the life-changing principle found in the passage that you believe God wants to implant in the hearts and minds of your group. The central idea answers the question, "What does God want us to learn from this passage?"

    c.   Provide one illustration that would make your central idea clear and meaningful to your group. This could be an illustration from your own life, or a story you've read or heard somewhere else.

    d.   Suggest one application that would help your group put the central idea into practice.

    e.   Choose an aim for your wrap-up talk. The aim answers the question, "What does God want us to do about it?" It encourages specific change in your group's lives, if they choose to respond to the central idea of the passage. Often it takes the form of a question you will ask your group: "Will you, will I choose to … ?"

9. Show up early to the study so you can arrange the room, set up the refreshments (if you are serving any), and welcome people as they arrive.

10. Whether your meeting includes a fellowship time or not, begin the discussion time promptly each week. People appreciate it when you respect their time. Transition into the discussion with prayer, inviting God to guide the discussion time and minister personally to each person present.

11. Model enthusiasm to the group. Let them know how excited you are about what you are learning—and your eagerness to hear what God is teaching them.

12. As you lead through the questions, encourage everyone to participate, but don't force anyone. If one or two people tend to dominate the discussion, encourage quieter ones to participate by saying something like, "Let's hear from someone who hasn't shared yet." Resist the urge to teach during discussion time. This time is for your group to share what they have been discovering.

13. Try to allow time after the questions have been discussed to talk about the "Apply what you have learned," "Think about" and "Personalize this lesson" sections. Encourage your group members in their efforts to partner with God in allowing Him to transform their lives.

14. Transition into the wrap-up talk, if you are doing one (see number 8).

15. Close in prayer. If you have structured your group to allow time for prayer, invite group members to pray for themselves and one another, especially focusing on the areas of growth they would like to see in their lives as a result of their study. If you have not allowed time for group prayer, you as leader can close this time.

16. Before your group finishes their final lesson, start praying and planning for what your next *Engaging God's Word* study will be.

COMMUNITY
BIBLE STUDY

Million+ people are engaging with God and His Word through CBS

Community Bible Study (CBS) is a global, interdenominational Bible study ministry offering a wide range of courses exploring various books of the Bible in both written and spoken formats, for all ages. Currently available in more than 85 languages, CBS Bible studies impact lives across more than 110 countries worldwide.

Since 1975, CBS has served as a conduit for the transformative power of God's Word; our participants study the Bible together in diverse settings, such as churches, prisons, schools, refugee camps, homes, coffee shops, and on the Internet. CBS is a participation-based ministry with trained leaders who foster in-depth, holistic engagement with God's Word within the context of a caring community, both in person and online.

The vision of Community Bible Study is, "Transformed Lives Through the Word of God."

The mission of Community Bible Study is, "To make disciples of the Lord Jesus Christ in our communities through caring, in-depth Bible Study, available to all."

CBS makes every effort to stand in the center of mainstream historic Christianity, concentrating on the essentials of the Christian faith rather than denominational distinctives. CBS respects different theological views, preferring to focus on helping people know God through His Word, grow deeper in their relationship with Jesus, and be transformed into His likeness.

Are you ready to go deeper in God's Word?

We would love to have you join us for an in-person or online CBS group. Scan the QR code to find a group.

For more information call 1-719-955-7777 or email info@communitybiblestudy.org.

Engage Bible Studies are available from Amazon and fine bookstores near you.

Scan the QR code to see all the available titles.

Made in the USA
Coppell, TX
19 August 2024